The Subject and Other Subjects

The Subject and Other Subjects
On Ethical, Aesthetic, and Political Identity

Tobin Siebers

Ann Arbor
The University of Michigan Press

Copyright © by the University of Michigan 1998
All rights reserved
Published in the United States of America by
The University of Michigan Press
Manufactured in the United States of America
⊚ Printed on acid-free paper

2001 2000 1999 1998   4 3 2 1

No part of this publication may be reproduced,
stored in a retrieval system, or transmitted in
any form or by any means, electronic,
mechanical, or otherwise, without the written
permission of the publisher.

A CIP catalog record for this book is available from the British Library.

Library of Congress Cataloging-in-Publication Data

Siebers, Tobin.
   The subject and other subjects : on ethical, aesthetic, and political identity / Tobin Siebers.
      p. cm.
   Includes bibliographical references (p.) and index.
   ISBN 0-472-09673-7 (acid-free paper)
   1. Self (Philosophy). 2. Subject (Philosophy). 3. Identity.
4. Aesthetics. 5. Ethics. 6. Political science—Philosophy.
7. Postmodernism. I. Title.
BD438.5.S54 1998
126—dc21
                                                        97-33948
                                                            CIP

Preface

It is a commonplace to define aesthetics as a mode of subjectivization originating with the Enlightenment. Aesthetics produces a certain kind of bourgeois subject or a certain kind of democratic subject, depending on which theoretical narrative you believe.[1] Oddly, however, an equivalent hypothesis does not exist for ethics and politics, even though they would seem to have more to do than aesthetics with questions of identity. Apparently, ethics and politics simply produce the same types of subjectivity as aesthetics. But if it is true, as Husserl said, that consciousness is always consciousness of something, then the object of consciousness matters. The self becomes conscious of itself through the mediation of its objects of consciousness, including other subjects. This is all the subject has. And yet it is never enough to explain what a subject is. My hope is that more diverse speculation about ethical, aesthetic, and political modes of representation will broaden our ideas about the strange interaction between subjects and objects and other subjects that characterizes subjectivization. How, specifically, does the aesthetic subject interact with the political and ethical one? How are their objects different? How do they use one another's resources, if they do?

These questions will, I hope, strike some of my readers as valuable. But other readers will want to resist them. The definitions of ethics, aesthetics, and politics have been rendered somewhat elastic, if

---

1. On the association between aesthetics and political subjectivization, see Luc Ferry (1993, 3), who associates aesthetics with democracy: "aesthetics is the field par excellence in which the problems brought about by the subjectivization of the world characteristic of modern times can be observed in the chemically pure state"; Terry Eagleton (1990, 3), who links art to bourgeois subjectivity: "The construction of the modern notion of the aesthetic artefact is thus inseparable from the construction of the dominant ideological forms of modern class-society, and indeed from a whole new form of human subjectivity appropriate to that social order"; and Hans-Georg Gadamer (1975), who links aesthetics and politics in a more politically neutral way.

Preface

not indistinguishable, by the last thirty years of critical and cultural analysis, and consequently any suggestion that we might want to restore a firmer sense of their differences will probably be greeted by skepticism. Indeed, a general distrust of definition is part of how we define critical and cultural analysis today; this tendency is obvious in many memorable slogans and significant ideas of recent years. On the political front, the slogan, "Everything is political," has rendered politically backward, if not futile, the gesture of defining politics apart from other modes of representation. Similarly, the critical emphasis on ethics in Wayne Booth, J. Hillis Miller, Bernard Williams, and others has made it difficult to conceive of the definitional limits of ethics. Williams (1985), for example, believes that ethics meets its limits only at the frontier of philosophy, while Miller conceives of the ethical as synonymous with language itself (1987, 1990). Often, for the person on the street, the attempt to posit a limit to ethics is thought to be unethical in itself. In the case of aesthetics, of course, the resistance to definition is less apparent, since no one has ventured lately to declare that everything is aesthetic, although once upon a time all the world was said to be a stage. Nevertheless, this exception appears to have more to do with the apparent irrelevance of art in many intellectual circles today than with any sense of shyness about making general and iconoclastic statements against definition.

If it were plausible that everything is political, or ethical, or aesthetic, we would need only to determine which phrase is most true, at which point we would find ourselves in the midst of an unprecedented theoretical clarity. But if everything is not political, ethical, or aesthetic, we abandon the work of definition at our peril. Thanks to recent developments in theory, especially concerning gender, race, class, and nationalism, we have become more canny about the importance of ethics, aesthetics, and politics in general and about their tendency to dominate the representational field in particular. It may now be time to build on this knowledge and to turn once again to the more humble and less iconoclastic work of definition. One of the reasons that I decided to undertake this book was to try to sort through the confusion produced by the current hatred of definition.

Definitions, however, are difficult to create and to maintain. This is both because different ideas cooperate and compete with each other and because those people who would need to reach consensus for the work of definition to be moderately successful also cooperate and compete with each other (usually the latter). For this reason, I do not expect that readers will agree with either my interest in definition or with the specific definitions that I will be proposing. All I can say

Preface

about potential objections is that I encourage them because this book will have no value whatsoever if readers are not focused intensely on the problem of definition itself, if they do not take part in the dialogue involved in asking at every point of reading whether a given idea or situation should or should not be housed under one of my master terms. I want to encourage speculation, not to impose a set of rigid definitions, and I invite my readers to participate in this task with me.

I will not launch into a set of detailed suggestions about ethical, aesthetic, and political identity here, since that is the subject of what follows. All I will offer is a foretaste couched in a bit of speculative prose. Ethics, aesthetics, and politics, I will be arguing, are particular modes of representing the repetition of experience, which is to say that they are different retellings and rereadings of it. Experience involves repetition, paradoxically, because "events" do not become significant unless they are repeatable, and yet the repeatability of the experiential is itself a threat to the significance of experience.[2] The task of ethics, aesthetics, and politics is to use narrative repetition against the repetition of experience; they are retellings that try to make of repetition a stable object of consciousness. Each mode helps the subject to imagine a particular kind of object, in effect producing an identity and goals compatible with it. But because subjectivities and goals overlap in certain situations, conflict and violence often result. This is a rather sad fact if one accepts as I do that these modes emerged in the first place as a way of deferring human conflict.[3]

Little discussion currently exists about the relation between human conflict and the distinctive modalities of ethical, aesthetic, and political representation. This is all the more surprising considering how overwhelming is the everyday preoccupation of human beings with human violence.[4] Each mode, however, may be said to address conflict in a distinctive way. The task of ethics is to resolve

---

2. That the significance of the experiential is based on its repeatability is the subject of "La Parole soufflée," where Derrida (1978, 170–75) makes the case that there is nothing to say about the "unique." The world is given significance, he argues, through a process of signification by which the rapidity of the oscillations of the unique are put into language and thereby achieve the status of "object," "subject," "event," "experience," etc.

3. My previous work has focused intensely on the relation between representation and human conflict (Siebers 1988, 1993), the earliest expositions being bound to genre studies (1983, 1984).

4. The one exception I know is the school of generative anthropology headed by Eric Gans (1993). Gans uses René Girard's views about human violence to establish a systematic theory of representation in which ethical, aesthetic, and political modes are given separate definitions.

Preface

conflict by configuring differences in terms of repetition or sameness; the modern appreciation of equality is its greatest achievement. When people fail in this task, as they often do, and see only the differences between themselves, they usually try to represent these very differences as objects of goodness, even though any new object of goodness will almost always end by reproducing familiar ethical conflicts. Whence the appearance of what I will call the nausea of ethics: human beings are disgusted by the fact that moral conflicts return ad infinitum and yet produce neither an accumulation of moral knowledge nor a vision of moral progress that is itself free of moral conflict. Aesthetics, of course, prefers good taste to nausea. Its object of the good is beauty—whatever can be appreciated. Aesthetics transcends the nausea of ethics by giving it a pleasing form, but the object of beauty remains in some way a suspicious entity, and many people are compelled, especially in intellectual circles, to expose the strangeness and violence lurking beneath its shimmering surface. Little else explains the distrust of beauty found today on the both the Left and Right. When either faction finds beauty, it expects to uncover ugliness. Finally, politics represents repetition in terms of community, which is an aesthetic object or artifact designed especially to provide a solution to ethical conflict, but politics makes the decisions necessary to create community in a way unacceptable to ethics in its purest form. Politics wants to produce as much consensus as possible by enticing individuals to embrace its vision of a beautiful "we," thereby requiring them to swallow their dissatisfaction for the chance to experience the pleasures of communal life. But the beholder of this beautiful "we" will always be tempted to imagine a "we" more beautiful and more inclusive, and so politics is forever troubled by the moral disgust of its citizens with existing political communities.[5]

---

5. Lyotard suggests that the limits to our understanding of "we" derive from the experience of the Holocaust: "If 'Auschwitz' has no name, is it not because it is the proper name of para-experience, that of the impossibility of forming the we? Is it not the case that in concentration camps there is no plural subject? And is it not further the case that for want of this plural subject, there can remain 'after Auschwitz' no subject which could presume to name *itself* by naming this 'experience'?" (Lyotard 1989b, 373). The idea that "we" reaches its limits because of the Holocaust is provocative. And yet could the Holocaust be construed as violent without our being able to see it in terms of the failure to achieve an inclusive vision? Our nausea with this violence already displays the moral sentiments whose origin Lyotard would ascribe to the Holocaust. No doubt, however, the Holocaust has in its role as ethical catastrophe portrayed like never before the horrors and consequences brought about by failing to think inclusively. In this sense, it has effected a sea change in moral consciousness comparable to only rare events in human history (the Lisbon earthquake, the French Revolution, and Hiroshima, to name a few others).

Preface

Human beings need to surmount repetition through narrative if they are to make anything of their individual selves and of their life together, and ethics, aesthetics, and politics may all in a sense be said to be forms of narrative whose by-products are particular subjects and objects. We seek emancipation from repetition in the retelling of stories, narrative being the homeopathic remedy for what ails us. The "function of narrative," as Roland Barthes understood, "is not to 'represent'"; "it is to constitute a spectacle still very enigmatic for us but in any case not of a mimetic order"; it arises from "the need to vary and transcend the first *form* given" to human beings, "namely repetition." Human beings, Barthes continues, "ceaselessly re-inject into narrative what they have known, what they have experienced; but if they do, at least it is in a form that has vanquished repetition and instituted the model of a process of becoming" (1977, 123–24). Narrative creates something that stands forth spectacularly not merely as an object but as a subject in the process of becoming itself or something else. That these objects and subjects may be graspable as models of the process of becoming exposes how self-contradictory they are, since it is difficult to imagine a symbol for something that is in the process of becoming something else.

I am less interested for my part, however, in pointing out the inherent instability of these subjects and objects, as has been the practice in critical theory for the last thirty years, than in speculating about the enigmatic dance of appearance and disappearance through which they manifest themselves. Such speculations introduce questions that cross and uncross the wires between ethical, aesthetic, and political representation, and they should make us curious about our basic assumptions about the terms. Is a person whom we consider to be an example of personhood still a person? What happens when we personify a thing? How does one person think from the perspective of a people? (Can one conceive of what it means to have the perspective of a people?) When a person is called beautiful, why does it strike us as an objectification? Does what we desire include the possibility of desiring otherwise, and if we accomplished this desire, would we see ourselves and our objects of desire differently? I warn that it is not always clear that speculation on these and similar questions makes sense. They are questions that confound us with sorrow and amazement and ecstasy, and yet they are part of the everyday experience of both subjects and objects. This is the experience that most interests me and why I return repeatedly to scenes where human beings and things become other than what they are or make their presence known or unknowable in spectacular ways.

Preface

The widespread skepticism about subjectivity (or, for that matter, objectivity) found everywhere today may be too robust to make a theoretical description of the subject viable any more, although I am obviously tempted by it. This skepticism is itself a product of history, naturally, which means that the chaotic path of subjectivization does have recognizable events, even though the cause and effect between history and the subject might seem more rhapsodic than constant. It is this very history that may explain, for example, why some thinkers find the notion of the subject itself to be so objectionable and why these same thinkers manage to amplify their own subjectivity by making the objection. The source of this objection is, in my opinion, an ethical critique of Enlightenment principles based itself on Enlightenment principles, and it almost always results in the paradoxical taking of the subject to a higher power of autonomy, autonomy being the Enlightenment's greatest invention. Thus, the freeing of the subject from subjectivity found in current thought is paradoxically cast as the greatest freedom that any subject can attain. Autonomy challenges our power to imagine the subject because it both insists on being seen as the defining feature of the self and denies that any self might adequately symbolize it. The free subject becomes "nothing" under the pressure of the idea of freedom—as the philosophical tradition spanning from Kant, through Hegel, to Sartre likes to phrase it—and yet nothingness is never adequate to what a self is; it is always less or more than its subject matter. For once the subject becomes "nothing," it has to turn around and make something of itself, if only to begin the process of self-abnegation once more. This is to say that we privilege freedom above all else—as well we should—but sometimes to the point of suspecting that freedom is itself the worst threat to freedom.

The increasing democratization of our world and the freedom from tradition that it entails have given to individual human beings an unprecedented autonomy, and yet they want more of it. These freedoms have taken the form of new rights and entitlements, and the continued liberation of human beings, which was the project begun by Enlightenment humanism, will no doubt produce more and more of them. It therefore behooves those of us who consider ourselves theoretically inclined to provide some discussion of subjectivity that might account for these transformations rather than taking the high moral road and denouncing subjectivity itself as an insult to freedom. Obviously, the progressive subjectivization of the world is the path by which human emancipation is occurring. This emancipation will not produce a utopia—although utopia is a good thing to keep in mind from time to time—since it will be, no doubt, as fraught with violence and confusion as other significant movements in history. Our wholly understandable fear of violence and confusion might tempt us to impose limits on freedom as a result. But once one realizes what freedom is, and if one believes, with the Enlightenment, that it is the destiny of the human race, then the choice is clear. Either one is in favor of emancipation or one is not.

Since my argument does not proceed chronologically but tries to speculate on questions that cross and uncross the wires of ethical, aesthetic, and political representation as we normally know them, it may be useful to provide a map of the territory for my readers. Chapter 1, "Ethics ad Nauseam," lays down my basic argument about conflict and the nausea of repetition and defines how ethics, aesthetics, and politics represent and stabilize them. It also explains that these modes use one another's resources, although I argue that the dominant mode remains the ethical because it is at once most concerned with the nature of subjectivity and closest to the problem of human conflict. Chapter 2, "What does Postmodernism Want? Utopia," applies some of the findings of the introduction to the problem of postmodernism, which I define as an aesthetic movement driven by the political desire for utopia. I also try to give the idea of postmodern desire greater amplitude by applying it to three specific case studies: cold-war politics, gender studies (or the romance of community), and the sculpture of Jackie Winsor. In chapter 3, "Multiculturalism, or the Ethics of Anti-Ethnocentrism," I show how multiculturalism confounds ethical and political points of view: the multicultural view of the world constantly confronts one with an idea of political community that is ethically unsatisfying, even though it is itself driven by the desire for ethical satisfaction. Chapter 4, "Reading for Character: Where It Was, I Must Come to Be," analyzes the work of J. Hillis Miller on prosopopoeia and explores the conflict between ethics and aesthetics, between "I" and "it," found in the dynamics of reading. Reading for character encourages a process of identification that at once builds the moral character of readers and threatens them with a sometimes deadly, aesthetic objectification. Chapter 5, "What Is There? A Dialogue on Obscenity, Sexuality, and the Sublime," further explores the objectification of the subject in the context of the much-discussed relation between sexuality and the sublime. One of my purposes here is to restore a political status to beauty and to explain why Freudianism and Heideggerianism have tended to give greater preference to the aesthetics of the sublime. My other purpose is to provide an analysis of the ways in which current philosophical models confront the spec-

Preface

tacular and unknowable apparition of "what is there," be it a subject, an object, or something in between. In chapter 6, "Politics and Peace," I redescribe ethics, aesthetics, and politics in the context of Kant's late political philosophy and experiment with my own definitions up to this point, the goal being to open up my method and to question my own conclusions. Finally, my conclusion, chapter 7, confronts the fact that objectification is central to human thought, despite the cruelty, injustice, and sacrifices involved in it, our ethical distaste with this fact being both sublime and idiotic.

Last but not least, I am grateful to Andrew McKenna and James Williams for inviting me to speak on these topics at Loyola University of Chicago and Stanford University, and to the editors of *American Literary History, Contagion, Michigan Quarterly Review, Semiotica,* and the University of Michigan Press for permission to reprint various materials, all of which have been revised. I also acknowledge the generosity of the Paula Cooper Gallery for granting permission to reproduce photographs of Jackie Winsor's sculpture, the support of the College of Letters, Science, and the Arts, especially of the Office of the Vice President for Research, and the kindness of the fellows and staff at the Institute for the Humanities, where I spent a wonderful year in residence.

Contents

1. Introduction: Ethics ad Nauseam
   1

2. What Does Postmodernism Want? Utopia
   29

3. Multiculturalism, or the Ethics of Anti-Ethnocentrism
   47

4. Reading for Character: Where It Was, I Must Come to Be
   77

5. What Is There? A Dialogue on
   Obscenity, Sexuality, and the Sublime
   95

6. Politics and Peace
   115

7. Conclusion
   131

References
137

Index
145

Introduction: Ethics ad Nauseam

One of the great temptations regarding ethics is to view it as cumulative, as if history provided the occasion to practice and to perfect our moral knowledge. History repeats itself, people say, because the idea of repetition is the necessary corollary to our desire to redirect old events toward better conclusions, to redeem failures of the past, and to refashion ourselves through the power of experience. Indeed, the concept of moral experience would be wholly incoherent if not for our belief that we will find ourselves again in similar circumstances.[1]

This idea of ethics, however, recoils from the most distasteful aspect of repetition, its nauseousness, by which I mean that we usually make the repetition of experience palatable by placing it in the service of either comic or tragic conclusions. Either repetition ensures our moral experience, despite a few setbacks, and thus historical progress—in short, it guarantees a happy ending—or it makes history into a tragedy in which we are condemned to witness the ceaseless replay of violence and destruction, without having the slightest chance of altering it. This more wicked sense of repetition—found in Nietzsche's concept of the eternal return or in Freud's repetition compulsion—is frightening, but it also satisfies our sense of drama. In other words, it is aesthetically pleasing. The two dominant senses of repetition, then, appear to provide us with the generic choice between playing in a comedy or in a tragedy. The ethical dilemmas of history will turn out to have been either a series of pratfalls and mistaken identities—laughably farcical—or a series of fatalistic and unfathomable riddles—utterly tragic. In any event, we will have been thoroughly entertained.

Marx has already played with these themes, of course, quipping

---

1. Because moral philosophy since Hegel has often tried to maintain a distinction between *ethics* and *morality*, I should note that I use these words interchangeably for the purpose of elegant (aesthetic) variation. See Siebers 1992 on the false distinctions between them.

that history does indeed repeat itself—the first time as tragedy, the second time as farce. But his view of repetition has little light to shed on the nausea of ethics; it only reveals that he saw repetition as aesthetic. Despite his apparent pessimism, Marx wanted a happy ending. If not, he would have at least described the second time of history as tragedy.

Ethics is nauseating because it involves repetition not in a comic or tragic sense but in the sense of the inescapable familiarity, intimacy, and redundancy of our dilemmas. The problems of ethics must be solved, but they cannot be solved. They return ad infinitum to the point where we are sick of thinking about them, and yet we must continue to think about them—we cannot help thinking about them. We search for different and better ways of representing the conflicts of ethics, but the better the representations, the more pleasing the forms, the less adequate they seem to the task. The metaphor of seasickness comes to mind. Like wave after wave against the bow of a ship, like the insufferable to-and-fro of a detestable motion, the conflicts of ethics provide no sense of an ending and no relief, only interminable repetition and the nausea that accompanies it.

Heidegger was right that ethics flourishes only when original thinking comes to an end, although his idea is framed from a perspective desirous of originality and thus aesthetic (1977, 195). At a certain point, ethics is about the inability to see differences: first, the differences needed to rationalize decisions; second, the differences that destroy human solidarity. The more ethical a thinker, the greater the tolerance for repetition and the greater the commitment to live with nausea.

Ethics

Ethics confronts the sickening repetition of conflict in human history. Etymology, of course, connects *ethics* to repetition, suggesting that ethics has always had something to do with recurring gestures, habits, nostalgic returns, and the repetition of experience.[2] In the modern world especially, we have reached the point where all the

---

2. In *The Nicomachean Ethics*, Aristotle traces the etymological development leading from the Greek verb meaning "to repeat" through nouns referring to "habitat," "habit," "character," and finally to "ethics." For an interesting commentary, see Lacan 1992, 10–12, where he claims that Freud breaks with the Aristotelian view of ethics. See also Siebers 1992, 5, 63–67.

Introduction

views in ethics look familiar.[3] One tendency has been to represent this effect as signaling an end: the end of time, the end of history, the death of the novel, and so forth. Would that it were true. It is more likely that we are condemned to repeat our gestures, conflicts, and arguments ad nauseam, running through the same maze, occasionally fooling ourselves that we have found a new path, finding again the same markers, coming upon our own footprints, discarded opinions, and old problems.

Postmodernism may be in part the awareness that we live in a world where repetition reigns. Recycling has become mandatory for the intellectual as well as the ecological world. In recent years, we have seen Michel Foucault return to Greek ethics to create a moral program for the postmodern world, Alasdair MacIntyre and Bernard Williams rediscover the value of Aristotle, and the resurgence of a neo-neo-Kantianism in the philosophies of John Rawls and Jean-François Lyotard. Rather than creating new systems or new master narratives, postmodernists become inveterate collectors, their intention being to reassemble old parts in new patterns. They seek relief from nausea in the compromised novelty of pastiche, parody, and ironic citation. Some of the descriptive terms used by theorists today—*patchwork, collage, quiltings, hybridity*—reveal only too clearly the collecting mentality at work in postmodernism.

Populist efforts in ethics only parody the academic theories (unless it is the other way around). The quest to recover lost values, family or otherwise, to turn back the clock on institutions, standards, and principles, and to restore senses of self and nation from bygone days are indications that we have lost hope of finding new solutions to old moral problems. We rummage through our mental attics and cellars, hoping to find some combination of old ideas that will produce something different. These efforts are often condemned by critics as nostalgic, but the desire to return to the past is driven less by nostalgia than by the sense that we cannot escape the past, that the future is in the past, and that we have already lived through it many times.

It is, of course, common in ethical theory today to remark upon the vertiginous complexity of moral argument and justification, although increasingly this complexity is attributed to moral rhetoric and not to the problems debated by ethics. Geoffrey Galt Harpham in *Getting It Right* illustrates the tendency in his analysis of Heidegger's politics, recognizing the relation between nausea and moral

---

3. Except in medical ethics, where technology introduces new dilemmas, although usually they are variations on traditional conflicts.

rhetoric. In 1938, Heidegger denounced Max Müller, a former student, to the university administration at Freiburg for being "unfavorably disposed" to National Socialism. When Müller confronted him, he explained that principle required him to tell the truth about Müller's politics. This episode is truly repugnant to moral sense not because Heidegger so easily excused his betrayal of a friend, although this is a factor, but because the two principles involved, truth-telling and loyalty to friends, are so worthy of preservation and yet have become in this situation mutually exclusive. Harpham, however, traces our disgust with this episode not to the conflict between these principles but to the difficulty of moral description: "How do we decide which principle ought to prevail when both principles can be so easily redescribed in terms of the other as a failure of principle? . . . The fact that the application of sound ethical principle to action cannot prohibit such acts as the betrayal of friends to Nazis is the nausea of ethics, that which it can neither reject nor swallow" (1992, 34).

Principles conflict in part because they are open to interpretation. More precisely, these interpretations often entail "redescriptions," where the emphasis lies on the repetition of a previous description under another description. The extravagant scene of ethical analysis, according to Harpham, is a site of "conversion" where one meaning constantly metamorphoses into its other. Harpham is correct that many statements can be redescribed as the justification for any number of moral positions. This perpetual redescription sets into motion the sickening repetition of ethical deliberation. But it may be more accurate to say that redescription is nauseating because it both preserves a sense of earlier meaning and produces conversions of meaning. Nausea rises up as a result of the rocking from one extreme of meaning to another.

It is one thing to recognize the repetition of ethical deliberation. It is another to attribute the nausea of ethics entirely to rhetorical repetition. For Harpham, contradictory meanings inhabit language like a cyst. But if there is a cyst in our language, it is a kernel of reality from which not even the most ceaseless driftings of signification can escape. Perpetual redescription exists as a phenomenon because *something* keeps happening—something that we would like to end. The lining up of descriptions under other descriptions produces narratives—aesthetic narratives—the purpose of which is to bring to a conclusion that conflict whose insistence first sparked a need for description. These narratives are plots against ethical conflicts and humiliations. They are utopian in their desire to solve these problems; they are

Introduction

dystopian in the recognition that resolving a conflict once will not prevent that conflict from reappearing, and that the solution to a conflict in the past will not necessarily resolve the same conflict when it recurs, as it inevitably must. Increasingly, because of these repetitions, postmodern ethics defines itself as dystopian, which is to say that it is an ethics skeptical about the possibility of ethics.

Another way of explaining this phenomenon is to recognize that repetition creates an intolerable temporal distortion. Psychoanalysis describes this temporal distortion as *Nachträglichkeit* or "retroaction." As one of the laws of desire, according to psychoanalysis, retroaction involves an interpretive process by which earlier events, which remain unconscious, are marked as sexual after the fact under the influence of later ones. For Jacques Lacan and his followers, however, retroaction takes on an ethical dimension because it connects time and moral experience: it creates a temporal lag between causes and effects, which makes the informed choice of actions extremely difficult. As John Rajchman describes it in *Truth and Eros,* "Events occur too early, or their effects come too late, for us to be able to 'assimilate' them in the portion of living that is governed by *proairesis* [choice]" (1991, 39).[4] The time of ethical goals is the future perfect: the time of "it will have been." When we propose an action to ourselves, we tend to read it retroactively from the perspective of a future end and to ask how that end relates to our personal history and hopes for it; goal-oriented behavior views actions in the present as causes for future effects, and we judge our actions according to these imagined ends. The nausea of ethical deliberation arises from the fact that we must replay the same action many times under different descriptions. At the present moment, I pose the all-consuming questions, "Where am I? What am I doing? Why?" The answer is "I am here doing this because it will have been the case that *x.*" I choose to act on this premise. But I cannot know in advance what I will seem to know all too well after the fact. For at some future date, another effect of the action is revealed to me, and I discover to my misfortune that an entirely different plot guided me. Twenty-five centuries of moral expe-

---

4. Not only do we have difficulty remembering events that we cannot regulate, we also have difficulty using the moral knowledge that we have acquired through experience. This is most obviously the case when we fail to understand our circumstances because we suffer from too little experience. We acquire with such experience the perception that we have won it too late, and we feel resentful as a consequence. It is less obvious, however, that we may possess too much moral experience too soon, harming ourselves and others because our knowledge is too great for the situation to bear.

rience have taught us that we know little more than the Greeks did about ethical cause and effect. The same laws of destiny—laws beyond human understanding—have been repeating themselves since time began.

No wonder, then, that postmodernists have sought relief from repetition in repetition. That they use repetition for ethical effect, however, is demonstrated by their use of emancipatory vocabulary. In *Gender Trouble*, for example, Judith Butler argues against static gender identity by adopting the idea of performance, which she defines as a "stylized repetition of acts" (1990, 140). She believes that repetition configures all identity but that we can nevertheless control *how* to repeat patterns of identity. Controlled repetition, for Butler, frees women from the bad effects of repetition: "To deconstruct the subject of feminism is not, then, to censure its usage, but, on the contrary, to release the term into a future of multiple significations, to emancipate it from the maternal or racialist ontologies to which it has been restricted, and to give it play as a site where unanticipated meanings might come to bear" (1992, 16). "Resignification," as Butler calls it, makes agency possible, for it enhances subjectivity and liberates it from positions of subordination. Parody, performance, and pastiche transgress stable identity by repeating it. They permit something new and unanticipated to emerge from the insufferable clichés of the past.

Donna Haraway's term for the same process is "feminist figuration." Her innovative combinations of feminine, animal, and machine metaphors—the stuff that cyborgs are made of—intend to produce new descriptions of human subjectivity in order to free us from established identities. Her target for attack, however, is explicitly characterized in terms of bad repetition, whereas feminist figuration represents good repetition:

> Figuration is about resetting the stage for possible pasts and futures. Figuration is the mode of theory when the more "normal" rhetorics of systematic critical analysis seem only to repeat and sustain our entrapment in the stories of the established disorders.... Feminist humanity must, somehow, both resist representation, resist literal figuration, and still erupt in powerful new tropes, new figures of speech, new turns of historical possibility. For this process at the inflection point of crisis, where all the tropes turn again, we need ecstatic speakers ... [speakers] who might figure the self-contradictory and

Introduction

necessary conditions of a nongeneric humanity. (Haraway 1992, 86)

Butler and Haraway are utopian theorists, and to their credit, but they cannot pretend to resignify history unless they make the leap of faith that repetition is revolutionary rather than reactionary. When postmodernists are able to sustain their faith in the revolutionary effect of repetition, they sound utopian, which is to say—I will be arguing—that they embrace aestheticism. When they reach the horrible conclusion that repetition is reactionary, they lose faith and make dystopian noises, which is another way to embrace aestheticism. Both conclusions tend to ignore the disgusting effect of repetition. The ethics of repetition is nauseous because repetition cannot be directed with any kind of consistency toward either revolutionary or reactionary ends. As Harpham persuasively concludes, theorists of emancipatory repetition, such as Butler and Haraway, maintain "a dubious faith in the capacity of repetition to open up politically progressive possibilities of agency and selfhood" (1992, 150). They believe that they can select and manage the effects of repetition. But repetition, Harpham argues, cannot "wholly transcend its own reactionary primariness, sublimating it without reserve" (150). In short, repetition is not *either* tragic *or* comic, *either* revolutionary *or* reactionary. It is also nauseatingly the same.

In some ways, postmodernists do live with the nausea of ethics. For their acceptance of some forms of repetition is also a way of refusing aesthetic and political closure. Indeed, they oppose closure to openness with a rhetoric that stresses the pluralism, proliferation, vertiginous signification, dissemination, undecidability, heterogeneity, hybridity, and reiterability of linguistic practices. The desires to remain at sea, to tolerate conflict, to embrace contradiction represent attempts to live with nausea. Postmodernists refuse closure because they associate it with an ethical crisis in which each and every just conclusion brings with it the disgusting return of injustice. But not even the most seasoned hand at ethical deliberation can remain at high sea forever, choking down again the same vomitory chunks of experience with each insufferable rocking of the ship of state. Nor would it be desirable, since both aesthetic and political history progress by coming to conclusions that are subsequently replaced by other conclusions. The autonomy of self-reflection endures as long as one remains at sea and suffers the nausea of ethics. Aesthetics and politics begin when self-reflection discovers an object other than itself or reaches a conclusion.[5] For both aesthetics and politics obey the need to bring an end to the nausea of ethics.

Aesthetics

Beauty as the Symbol of Morality

Ethics and aesthetics can be distinguished in the Kantian definition according to their representations of autonomy. In ethics, autonomy refers to the freedom of the subject to test the contradictions between maxims of action. What Thomas Nagel calls "the view from nowhere," Bernard Williams names the "mid-air position," and Kant labels "autonomy" permits the self-reflective subject simultaneously to occupy a position and to reflect upon that position from a distance. Or, to use Kant's most accessible image, it creates a situation in which the person accused by the court of conscience is one and the same person with the judge of the court: "a twofold personage, a doubled self who, on the one hand, has to stand in fear and trembling at the bar of the tribunal which is yet entrusted to him, but who, on the other hand, must himself administer the office of judge" (1971, 104n).[6] No

---

5. Cornelius Castoriadis's remarkable description of this process bears repeating:

> What is it that I ought to think (about being, about *physis*, about the *polis*, about justice, etc.—and about my own thinking)? This questioning goes on, and has to go on, incessantly, for a simple reason. Any being-for-itself exists and can only exist in a *closure*—thus also society and the social individual. Democracy is the project of breaking the closure at the collective level. Philosophy, creating self-reflective subjectivity, is the project of breaking the closure at the level of thought. But of course, any breaking of the closure, unless it remains a gaping "?" which does not break anything at all, posits something, reaches some results, and, thereby, risks erecting again a closure. The continuation and renewal of reflective activity—not for the sake of "renewal," but because this *is* self-reflective activity—entails therefore the putting into question of previous results (not necessarily their rejection—no more so than the revisability of laws in a democracy entails that they have to be changed wholesale every morning). (1991, 21)

6. This image is of course aesthetic. In fact, Kant refers such images and representations of character to an aesthetics of morals. The notion of the "split subject," popular among postmodernists, is similarly an aesthetic device created to endure the nausea of repetition. It is an attempt to represent moral autonomy without repeating the dreaded vocabulary of autonomy. Consider, for example, descriptions of the split subject with regard to the dilemma of essentialism. Postmodernists often advocate a "strategy" or "performance" of essentialism, which embraces essentialistic rhetoric to advance political agendas, while placing it simultaneously in doubt. The subject

Introduction

one, according to Kant, is capable of understanding how this inscrutable autonomy works. Freedom is incomprehensible, he says, although we comprehend its incomprehensibility. It may be clearer to say that moral autonomy cannot be understood because it cannot be conceived of as an object. Paradoxically, freedom must be objectified to be represented, but the objectification of freedom puts such constraints on it that it is no longer recognizable as freedom.

In aesthetics, however, objects exist, and they are beautiful. Aesthetic representation evokes the subjective response called beauty. Free beauty is nevertheless as impossible to describe as moral autonomy, according to Kant, for it cannot obey a rule and still preserve its capacity for giving pleasure. The art object commands inexplicably the recognition of its beauty. This beauty is nevertheless objectified. It exists somewhere. It is identifiable with the work of art, even though it can be maintained that beauty is not really *there*, that it rises miraculously out of the materiality of the object, hovering over it or casting its aura about it. Kant refers to this mysterious effect as symbolism. Symbolism is the process by which the moral autonomy of the subject is projected upon an object and experienced there as beautiful. Beauty is the symbol of morality, Kant concluded, giving heavy emphasis to the symbolism (1952, §59). Beauty permits a mediated experience of moral autonomy. It grounds the groundless experience of self-reflection.

If Kant was right about ethics and aesthetics, aesthetic pleasure replaces momentarily the need for ethical satisfaction. Sickened by the infinite regress of moral reflection and the disgusting repetition of experience, we seek repose in the aesthetic object of taste. The stress in taste is always on objectification because aesthetic pleasure serves to put ethical dissatisfaction into a form that can be swallowed. Current efforts to relate ethics to the aesthetics of the sublime resist such objectification—no doubt for all the reasons that make "objectification" a derogatory concept today—but the sublime is no more successful in expressing the nausea of ethics than the representation of beauty. The sublime merely defines the aesthetic moment at which autonomy is objectified in a consciousness superior to its own. The

---

maintains the split between strategic and real essentialism, suffering the contradiction. When confronted by the doubt that strategic essentialism might be impossible for any subject to maintain, however, most postmodernists will admit that they cannot rectify the two times of essentialism and nonessentialism. Sooner or later performing essentialism makes one an essentialist. In the final analysis, notions such as the split subject and strategic essentialism are aesthetic devices used to express the utopian desire that we might find a solution to the nausea of ethics. They are examples of wishful thinking, although no doubt of the most admirable kind.

objectification is weaker than that found in the aesthetics of beauty, which is to say that it is more difficult to represent, but it remains a representation nevertheless. Indeed, it is most recognizably a variation on tragic representation. One exception is the infrequent emphasis among postmodernists on what Kant calls the mathematical sublime (1952, §26). It sometimes comes close to accepting nausea, but only in those forms that stress the tedious repetition of number strings rather than incomprehensibly large sums. The sublime represents an aesthetic moment fallen under the shadow of the insistent self-reflection of ethics, but it remains an aesthetics in the final analysis: like beauty, it compels moral self-reflection to project its own presence to another location, thereby breaking the redundant pattern of its deliberations and giving it relief from its own rationality. The sleep of reason does not produce monsters. It creates works of art.

Perhaps an example from a different domain may make the relationship between repetition and objectification clearer. An analogous situation arises in psychoanalytic treatment. According to Lacan, patients resist the initial transference to the analyst, especially when it is a matter of reliving an especially powerful trauma. The session returns patients to a scene of conflict, but they resist replaying the conflict both because it is unpleasurable to relive and because it requires that they transfer their emotions to the analyst, which is also a form of repeating the conflict. Consequently, at certain moments, Lacan explains, usually when the patients are experiencing conflicts most powerfully, resistance engulfs the session in the form of a paralyzing silence, and patients refuse to talk about their traumas. Instead, they objectify the resistance, turning their speech to an object in the room, most frequently to an object associated with the analyst's person: "the analyst's style or face, or his furniture" (1991, 40). The patients' disgust with their recurring trauma, with the trauma that has become the "transference," compels them to seek relief in the contemplation of an object, although the choice of the object betrays the influence of the transference. Nevertheless, the contemplation of the object affords them a moment of aesthetic pleasure that counteracts the nausea of repetition. It momentarily puts the conflict to rest by incorporating it in an object having visible qualities—a color and texture, a top, sides, and a bottom, a beginning and end. These qualities can be discussed and appreciated. Lacan, of course, does not recommend allowing patients to enjoy these moments of aesthetic repose. Analysts, he counsels, should return talk about their person, style, and possessions to the transference, that is, to symbolic repetition.[7]

---

7. Lacan in fact defines the ethics of psychoanalysis in terms of an opposition

Introduction

Style and Narrative

I will refer to *style* all claims made for aesthetic or ethical distinction based on the apparently objective qualities of modes of expression, especially of writing. Reconsider Lacan's description of the analyst's "style" as an obstacle to repetition. The style of the analyst represents in the patient's mind an aesthetic artifact summoned by the dissatisfaction of ethical deliberation. It permits the patient to focus on a difference when the rigors of transference offer only sickening repetition. Of course, the style of the analyst may also come to represent his or her moral superiority for the patient, since it symbolizes what is different about the analyst. Lacan does not link the idea of style preferentially to either aesthetics or ethics, since it does not make much sense to distinguish between them in this particular case. Clearly, the style of the analyst serves aesthetic and ethical ends.

It is nevertheless the case on the current theoretical scene that style has been almost entirely assimilated to ethics and not to aesthetics. Lacan's style is directed toward the problem of "beauty" in living, by which he attempts to rectify the contradictory requirements of culture and *jouissance*—the first being concerned with a form of the good, the second involving what is good for nothing (cf., Rajchman 1991, 70). Richard Rorty has argued that Derrida should be seen primarily as a stylist who is intent on creating beautiful new forms of writing that permit him to distance himself from the ethical conundrums of political culture, and Derrida has himself done a great deal to stimulate interest in matters of form by reinterpreting Nietzsche's moral thought as a stylistics.[8] Just as the aesthetic object comes to symbolize the unfathomable nature of moral autonomy in Kantian thought, style objectifies and beautifies the paradoxical repetitions of ethical deliberation. Indeed, *style* is most often defined today as a

---

between the Thing and symbolic repetition. The Thing *(das Ding)* is a kernel of the real, an objectification, a chunk of ego that becomes a fortress in which the patient may hide. The symbolic, however, represents the vertiginous domain of social contract, kinship, and arbitrary communication. To live in the symbolic, in the signifying chain, is to live at sea but also to live more fully. The ethics of psychoanalysis requires that the analyst help to free patients from their attachments to static ego formations and to give themselves over to the endless, though dizzying, possibilities of speech (1992, chaps. 2, 4–5, 8, 28).

8. On Derrida's love of the beautiful, consider Richard Rorty's appraisal: "Derrida is coming to resemble Nietzsche less and less and Proust more and more. He is concerned less and less with the sublime and ineffable, and more and more with the beautiful, if fantastical, rearrangement of what he remembers" (1989b, 136). On Nietzsche as stylist, see Derrida 1979.

mode specifically designed to deal with moral, political, or philosophical problems. "Perhaps to start to think is," John Rajchman explains in typical fashion, "to find oneself in a peculiar difficulty one knows not yet how to define. And the problem of 'style' in a philosophy is the problem of finding the words and the acts appropriate to the difficulty one thus discovers or brings to light" (1991, 26).

What does it mean, however, to invent a style appropriate to a conflict when this conflict follows the loathsome laws of repetition? It is certainly true that we desire different styles. They provide moments of relief and repose, and we should applaud their creation. While these moments are not resolutions in the strict sense of the word, they nevertheless appear to us as resolutions, resolutions that we desperately need. They are the utopian moments required to go on living in a world where utopia is what is most desired even if least probable. But ethical conflict cannot be stylized and know itself. It can only be repeated ad nauseam. Any style recognizable as a style, that is, as a characteristic difference, would fail to express the tedium of endless repetition. The desire to invent a style appropriate to ethical conflict obeys in the final analysis the desire to stylize conflict.

Today many theorists interested in the ethics of narrative find ways to stylize conflict, even though they claim that the most important task is to allow it to exist. A brief genealogy is easy to sketch. Derrida was among the earliest when he coined the word *différance* for the contradictory impulses of narrative to create differences and to defer them endlessly. Instructively, the word was an example of the phenomenon that it was invented to describe because the silent *a*, which insinuates the process of deferral into that of differing, cannot be tracked phonetically. This beautiful *a* teases the reader out of thought and comes to symbolize the mysterious combination of difference and deferral in Derrida's theory. Derrida soon found other words to represent the same effect: the proper name, hymen, supplement, margin, and so forth.

Paul de Man named the phenomenon in its ethical context "ethicity." Ethics, for de Man, seems to designate the structural interference between two distinct value systems (1979, 206). In fact, he claims, "ethics (or, one should say, ethicity) is a discursive mode among others" (206), which means that it obeys the laws of textuality. Ethicity, for de Man, is a term that emphasizes the textual nature of ethics, and a text never gives one value power over others. Thus, ethics does not ultimately differ from other textual modes: "The paradigm for all texts consists of a figure (or a system of figures) and its deconstruction" (205). Ethicity, in effect, stylizes conflict according to a linguistic

Introduction

model, suggesting that distinctions asserted in moral argument cannot be sustained at the level of language. Apparently dissatisfied with this general concept, de Man found specific ideas that possessed the quality of ethicity and could be given as examples: the rhetorical question, the dialogic, and so forth.

J. Hillis Miller, following de Man's lead, defined the ethics of reading in terms of even more specific examples of ethicity. In the case of Kant, the word *Achtung* represents the knife-edge between respect and fear, and thus the flimsy distinction upon which his ethical thought will stand or fall (1987, 19). The words *host* and *guest*, Miller claims, trip up M. H. Abrams's attempts to establish a moral hierarchy between criticism and literature (1977). Bartleby the Scrivener did not by accident discover the obnoxious phrase, "I would prefer not to." The word *preference*, according to Miller, belongs to a group of words especially fitted to deconstruction (1990, 154–55). Miller searches for the exact places in narratives where meaning is simultaneously asserted and denied. He ends by reducing most problems of interpretation to single words, so that narrative becomes not the telling of various events but the story of one word and its qualities (Siebers 1992, 28–32).

Meanwhile, in France, Jean-François Lyotard was developing a reading of the grand narratives of history and politics in terms of the rhetoric of *différance*. According to Lyotard, political and moral arguments may be summarized as "phrases in dispute," and no matter how much effort is put into reconciling phrases, a remainder of the dispute will always be left over after the parties in the conflict go away satisfied. He calls this remainder the *différend*. It locates the point in judgments, negotiations, and arbitration where disagreement is ignored so that people may agree to agree, although Lyotard is careful to note that différends point endlessly to other différends. The différend marks the existence of conflict within consensus. It is what master narratives cannot incorporate and still remain master narratives. Lyotard's theory is itself a masterful description of how agreements are formed and conflicts are stylized, and I do not dispute his picture of their micropolitics. But it makes no more sense to theorize about a phrase where disagreement exists than it does to argue that consensus is the result of having found one phrase in which all demands harmonize with each other. The idea of the différend seeks, if only in theory, to describe a fulcrum of meaning, but when we try to locate such fulcrums in a specific text, what we actually do is to create an aesthetic object to represent the conflict troubling us.

To represent conflict as an aesthetic object is to stylize conflict.

The Subject and Other Subjects

These artifacts are easier to grasp than the conflicts they represent, and they are less nauseating. A similar but perhaps necessary urge lies behind efforts to cleanse narrative of value judgments. Derrida intends, in Geoffrey Harpham's words, "to respect the epistemological moment that precedes any value judgment" (1992, 151). Yet it is not clear, as Harpham also points out, that epistemology can precede judgment, since a field of meaning innocently lacking value is not very epistemological. Attempts to describe an epistemological moment preceding judgment, value-free domains of textuality, and similar notions obey an ethical impulse but use aesthetic means to express it. They imagine a beautiful landscape at the moment before we mar it with our humanity. They strive to capture the pure surface upon which our impure values and judgments rest. The ultimate ethical desire, it appears, is to purify ethics of differences, values, conflicts, and judgments—to visualize the ethical ground, the ethical clay, out of which we mold our feet.[9]

Narrative repeats the repetition of experience, but it may also mimic this repetition without representing its nausea. Narrative, when least repressive, represents the repetition of experience as the endless sameness of ethics; when more repressive, it creates the infinite beauty of aesthetics. Reading is ethical in its conception that narrative replays the nauseous repetition of experience and ethical deliberation about it. Reading is aesthetic in its attempts to represent the repetition of experience or the nausea of ethics in a specific figure, word, or plot. But the nausea of ethics cannot be so located. All we can do is retell or reread the story one more time.

Imagine visiting a picture gallery of moral conflicts and being endlessly surprised by the novel forms, by the variety of the ethical, in the same way that one is endlessly surprised in an art gallery by the astonishing variety of beautiful forms. What a noble vision! But how futile! I hope that I am not being cynical when I contest such visions. I am

---

9. The attempt is nevertheless understandable, which is why I repeat it in my description of the conditions of possibility of ethics as repetition. Another way of framing the same problem is to note that the execution of a general concept appears purely formal when specific interpretations do not exist. This is why we need aesthetic experience to symbolize it. Harpham (1992), for example, tries to define the ethical precondition of ethics in terms of "imperativity." For him, the essence of ethics is to create and to follow imperatives, but imperativity leads to dissatisfaction because a particular application always appears less perfect than the general imperative. Consequently, Harpham's notion of imperativity remains purely formal because any example of it is necessarily an aesthetic artifact, and this artifact cannot exemplify the purity of imperativity as such without destroying it. In this sense my picture of unrelenting repetition uninterpreted is also formal.

Introduction

trying to appreciate aesthetic experience for what it is. What else can one do with it? If progress in ethics does exist, it exists because aesthetics is so little interested in progress of the same type, thereby creating the possibility of replacing the nausea of ethics with an aesthetics of morals. Aesthetics cares not whether the most recent form to emerge follows logically from the last. It is little interested in justice and missteps. Indeed, it cares most about being dissociated from or surmounting previous forms. (It never succeeds, but it always surprises us.) Aesthetics is interested only in the new.[10]

Those who would quest for a new style to deal with our moral problems are looking for beauty. There is, finally, one answer to the question, "Is there anything new in ethics?" There is nothing new in ethics. There is only something new in aesthetics and politics.

Politics

Ethos as Eros

Postmodern attempts to define ethics on the basis of style rather than law, on erotics rather than truth, on pleasure rather than knowledge share a utopian vision of repetition. The repetitiveness of the sexual act feels good. Encore! At last we have discovered a place where repetition is pleasurable. History repeats itself a third time as sex. History is the history of sexuality. At the same time, the imbecilic redundancy of sex requires style—style as law, as fashion, and as variation on a

---

10. Some may argue that art has ended because newness is no longer possible in the posthistorical era. Arthur Danto, for example, notices that postmodernists have given up the ambition to make art new: "What the end of art means is not, of course, that there will be no more works of art. If anything, there has been more art-making through the last decade than in any previous period of history. What has come to an end, rather, is a certain narrative, under the terms of which making art was understood to be carrying forward the history of discovery and making new breakthroughs" (1992, 10). This is a good description of the current state of the artworld, but it underestimates the extent to which each work of art, even though it may not be a theoretical breakthrough, strikes the beholder as new because of its status as an object. Unless a work of art explicitly reveals its own unoriginality (and even when it does— pace Warhol's *Brillo Box*), its form, integrity, and materiality grant to it a unique existence; it is viewed, whatever its borrowings from other forms and objects, as a new thing on the face of the earth. Consequently, the greater our sense of the nauseous repetition of moral existence, the more we desire the aesthetic repose provided by new works of art, and the more time we devote to art making. Anyone can become an artist today because everyone needs to be one. When the end of ethics comes into view, art does not die; it comes to life. From now on, we may expect art to become increasingly more popular and to see even more time devoted to aesthetic experience.

practice. Our culture abounds with manuals instructing us about new sexual styles, techniques, and gadgets. Better sex supposedly comes with more knowledge of the body, a better understanding of our partners, and more work. Get into shape. Make sex endlessly novel for yourself but consider your partner's feelings at the same time. Do not do anything to hurt other people, unless, of course, they want to be hurt.[11] These are some of the imperatives of the new sexual politics.

The attempt to transfer the scene of ethics from the city or individual self-reflection to the romantic couple seems, at first glance, to be only a sexualization of the idea of friendship, which has been since Greek times the major trope used to consider the political dimension of ethics (consider, for example, Aristotle's *allos auto*). The difference, often sexual, between self and other merely replaces the agon of Aristotelian friends or the split consciousness of Kantian autonomy.[12] Yet the shift to the sexual couple has changed the landscape of politics. First, feminism recognizes that ethical conflict requires political solutions, and its emphasis on the ethics of the couple has illuminated the interpersonal—the political—dimension of moral reflection. Second, the insistence by feminists and postmodernists on the political nature of matters usually considered private, most notably sex, has enlarged our understanding of what makes something politically important and of how certain issues are excluded from the public sphere. The slogan "The personal is the political" has had mixed results for feminism and postmodernism because it has so often rationalized a fascination with private fantasy and a disinclination to participate in the political process, but it has at least performed the service of requiring new definitions of the political.

The Political Is Artifactual

The new sexual politics transfers ethical deliberation to a more interpersonal and political scene rather than following the trend toward more individual expression that began with liberal individualism and culminated in phrases such as "The personal is the political." It has been less successful, however, in recognizing that politics is artifactual, by which I mean that politics requires aesthetic forms—of which facts are among the most important—to make progress. We generally prefer to contemplate the "beauty" of a solution rather than to con-

---

11. On the fallacy of this argument, see chap. 5.

12. The self of the self and the self of the other both contain within themselves the traditional self and other of self-reflective subjectivity. The number of players has doubled to two, while the dimension of consciousness has increased fourfold. The new politics of sex describes an orgy of moral reflection.

Introduction

tinue living with the nausea of our dilemmas. New political solutions, which do exist, only exist, first, because people agree to create such solutions and, second, because they agree to accept them, thereby putting aside ethical dissatisfaction. We agree to agree only to move to new ground, to experience new forms of agreement, and to create new communities. New communities also exist, which is to say that there is something aesthetic about them. Political forms are not natural; they are artificial. We create them just as we create works of art.

Although postmodern thinkers usually accept the idea that politics is artificial, they are less likely to believe that this artificiality is good. No postmodernist would think to criticize an aesthetic object for its artificiality, and yet artifice is seen as a severe limitation in the case of political forms, which suggests that postmodern politics still clings to a naturalistic fallacy. According to Hannah Arendt, however, politics is and must be what I have called artifactual. Indeed, her distinction between the public and private spheres, for which she has often been criticized, requires a strong awareness of the aesthetic nature of politics. Arendt enumerates three features of the public sphere, and each one reveals an artifactual dimension.[13] First, she insists that political activities are constructed rather than natural, which means that equality, justice, and human rights are defined and justified on the basis of consensus. The right to have rights is only recognized and safeguarded within a community. Politics always stresses the perspective of commonality; it defines a realm in which we recognize ourselves and others as participants in a community, and in which we consent to preserve that form of life (1958, 50). Politics requires a conception of form, according to Arendt, and she consequently honored rather than disdained the artificiality of public life.

Second, Arendt argued for the importance of a spatial and architectural conception of the public sphere. She viewed politics as a public activity, insisting that one cannot be part of the political process without being in some way present in a public space (1968, 220–21). Government buildings, monuments, and town squares make the public sphere present to its participants, even though these artifacts cannot be said in any sense to constitute it because a public space comes into existence, according to Arendt, only when individuals agree to act in concert. Rather, political spaces and architectural forms embody and represent our desire for a common political life in the same way

---

13. Margaret Canovan isolates these three features of Arendt's political philosophy in "Politics as Culture" (1985), and Maurizio Passerin d'Entrèves has enlarged upon them in "Hannah Arendt and the Idea of Citizenship" (1992). Both essays make valuable contributions to the definition of politics.

that works of art symbolize individual moral autonomy. We refer to public buildings and spaces as symbols of our desire for justice, equality, and human rights. They are artifacts that help us to contemplate these more elusive and enigmatic concepts.

Third, Arendt views the world itself as a necessary feature of the public sphere. Politics involves a world held in common by its participants, which means that they are concerned with the forms of life—the world—created by politics. But Arendt's idea of the world also includes the materiality of the world—its ecology. Notions such as public good define a common good that is not completely created by political communities. It describes the world as a good held in common, but Arendt stresses that we hold this world in common without owning it (1977, 104). Our first duty is to preserve the world, for there will arise many instances when our duty to preserve it will contradict actions and interests beneficial or profitable to our private existence. Greater profit, interest, and intimacy won at the cost of worldlessness produce only barbarism in Arendt's mind (1955, 13). Of first importance is the preservation of the world, and this task requires a disinterested and long-term appreciation of its physical qualities. It requires that we view the world as an aesthetic object whose beauty we are fortunate to experience and committed to protect.

Freedom of Speech

The example of free speech may serve to illustrate further the artifactual nature of political forms as well as their dependence on the distinction between public and private spheres. The right to free speech was created in the public sphere in order to guarantee the facility of expression needed to create again that sphere. To say that free speech is a creation is to maintain the idea that it involves an aesthetic experience. To argue that it requires a reciprocal relationship with the public sphere to thrive is to recognize that it is a political artifact that loses its function without the distinction between the public and private. Like all rights, free speech is created by communal agreement, and it therefore requires public spaces. Its original usage was strictly political since free speech empowers individuals in the community to make decisions about their common affairs.[14] Free speech is necessary

14. Notice that I am assuming that the political comes into existence on the basis of agreement created by individuals. Ernesto Laclau has made the case that the private is only a "residual category" (Miami Theory Collective 1991, 95), his point being that all individuals are only individuals qua political beings. Being a methodological holist, Laclau sees any category that does not remain at the level of collective representation as a residue. Being a methodological individualist, I quite natu-

Introduction

for the emergence of democracy; indeed, its appearance, even when spontaneous, is an incipient form of democracy. Democracy is the public form of government par excellence because it asserts that the political realm belongs to everyone. It also embraces the idea that people understand best the political process. Cornelius Castoriadis expresses it well: "There are not and cannot be 'experts' on political affairs. Political expertise—or political 'wisdom'—belongs to the political community" (1991, 108). Once the public sphere emerges, politics ceases to be the private affair of "the king, the priests, the bureaucracy, the politicians, and the experts" (112).[15] There emerges a world of contradictory, redundant, and boisterous discourse about community by which community is created.

It has sometimes been argued that the distinction between the public and private spheres is wholly artificial and cannot be maintained. This is true insofar as the distinction is created and created anew by free speech and therefore requires a political consensus to keep it intact. An awareness of the artifactual nature of politics is crucial to the existence of political life because it decrees the self-instituting power of consensus. This awareness is also the greatest threat to political life because it requires participants in politics to contemplate its arbitrary character. The public sphere is the most tenuous of realms because it requires the passionate but disinterested participation of a great many individuals in the community, but this contradictory imperative of passion and disinterestedness is not easily accepted by the majority of people.[16] Politics commands a passionate pursuit of ends that do not profit individuals in the short term, and it often

---

rally see things the other way around. In my opinion, the public is a supplemental creation, an artifact, to which people lend their individual support, thereby making consensus possible.

15. Rajchman, following Foucault, makes the case that free speech does not require a public sphere by arguing that it exists in the opinions given to kings by advisors (1991, 119–20). This argument fails for two reasons. First, it reduces free speech to the speech of experts who deny the free circulation of argument among the people purportedly to save the people from their own ignorance. Second, Foucault's example is naive. One cannot talk to a king in private. A king is a public figure by virtue of the fact that his power derives, despite all efforts to naturalize it in genealogy, from the community's support of his reign—a fact dramatized all too well by the violence of the French Revolution.

16. Castoriadis presents what might be considered a defining example of disinterestedness taken from Aristotle's *Politics:* when the governing body deliberates on whether to go to war with a neighbor, the representatives of the frontier zone are not allowed to vote because they cannot vote without their individual interests overwhelming their decision, whereas the decision has to be made on the basis of the common good of the entire community (1991, 111). "Imagine," Castoriadis asks, "the

requires these passionate individuals to put aside their passion for the common purpose at a moment's notice to preserve the common purpose. The public sphere is a space of tragedy, but of a tragedy of individuals, because it places constraints on individual behavior with the promise of celebrating an individual's virtue if he or she should accept these constraints, but it often causes individuals to lose their virtue in the very process of striving to be good. In short, the public sphere asks individuals to sacrifice themselves.

The sacrifice of individuals to public life is most visible in the case of free speech. Free speech requires individuals to speak their minds about the common ends of their community, but individuals, and not the community, bear the responsibility for this speech. No doubt, this frightening requirement has contributed to the transformation of free speech in the modern day. Free speech no longer refers exclusively to the right to have one's say about matters political. It has ceased to be the guarantee for a public sphere necessary to facilitate debate about common goals. Freedom of speech has now deteriorated into "freedom of expression," a phrase whose meaning exposes the disintegration of the distinction between public and private life in democratic society. In a sense, individuals have decided to speak their minds about only themselves so as not to bear responsibility for matters not of their own private concern. Freedom of speech presupposes a public sphere and a common pursuit, and it requires individuals to risk their opinions about public life and its goals in public. Freedom of expression views the public sphere in terms of publicity, and it uses the public domain to circulate entertainments, advertising, and pornography. Freedom of expression comes into existence by privatizing and depoliticizing the public sphere; it transforms a space created for political purposes into a commercial space where people and products are marketed.

The risk of this transformation, however, is built into the artifactual nature of politics. Because we create the public sphere by agreement, we may also transform that sphere by agreement or by consenting with our silence to changes made by other individuals and subgroups in the community. If individuals and small groups turn the subject of free speech away from the conditions of public life to other

---

following disposition in the U.S. Constitution: 'Whenever questions pertaining to agriculture are to be decided, senators and representatives from predominantly agricultural States cannot participate in the vote'" (1991, 111–12). Interest, then, is characterized in terms of the imagined position of the community, and disinterestedness in personal motives becomes a precondition for the individual to enter debates in the public sphere. Obviously, this type of thought takes a heavy toll on the individual.

Introduction

topics, and if the community does not agree to return their speech to its proper subject, the public sphere changes in character.

The change in the public sphere may be explained in part by the fascination with, and need of politics for, aesthetic experience. The political is susceptible to the aesthetic desire to use increasingly personal and idiosyncratic materials in pursuit of novelty and to create new forms at any cost because it needs new solutions and new forms of community to survive. Politics has a love-hate relationship with the aesthetic. Politics relies on the resourcefulness of personal experience and encourages its representation in art and other forms, for only by acquiring meaning may personal experience become public. "The experience as experienced, as lived, remains private," as Paul Ricoeur explains it, "but its sense, its meaning, becomes public" (1976, 16). But politics also needs to yoke private desires and energy to a common purpose, which means that the public sphere needs to discriminate between more private forms of expression because only those that contribute to the self-instituting power of the community are useful.

Aesthetic theory will never be able to distinguish between art and pornography because aesthetics has not the slightest interest in such differences. Aesthetics is only interested in whether an art form created by one person can affect another person. It is for political debate to decide which forms of expression are to be approved—and labeled art—and which are to be disapproved—and labeled pornography. For the forms of expression included in the public sphere have an immediate impact on the kind of community that it is in the process of affirming. For example, to approve of a possible community characterized by the kinds of behavior and ideals found in pornography is, for the political mind, to legislate that we live in that kind of community.[17] The political mind sees all forms of speech as a direct commentary on the type of community that we should be creating.

Sexual Intercourse

The greatest challenge to the distinction between public and private spheres in modern America has come from feminism. It is a legitimate challenge, and it requires serious thought and discussion. Feminists have charged that the idea of the public sphere promulgates styles of speech, reasoning, and discourse not available to every one who should be allowed by rights to participate in political life. Most

---

17. Sheila Jeffreys accurately sums up the political community imagined by pornographers. "Pornography is not egalitarian and gender free. It is predicated upon the inequality of women and is the propaganda that makes that inequality sexy" (1992, 465).

notable, definitions of politics that rely wholly on a notion of the public sphere hinder women from becoming full members of the community because their activities are relegated to the enclosed and private world of home and family. Traditionally men have shaped law in the public sphere of shared institutions, while women have created a intimate world conducive to the nurturing of children and domestic relationships. It has often been decreed by feminists and old-guard sexists alike that women's perspectives are not compatible with politics. The disinterestedness of political debate, for example, may strike women as indifference to important emotions and problems (Gilligan 1982, 22). No feminists are arguing, however, that gender differences should disqualify women from politics. For them, the idea that community requires a public sphere acts to exclude women from political power, and they have attacked the requirement with great energy in a variety of ways, demanding that the nature of politics itself be transformed.

Nevertheless, the women's movement has been more successful so far in raising women's self-esteem than it has been in its battle for equal wages and political representation, although some legislation against sex discrimination has emerged. This is the case because there is much resistance to political reform from men in power, and it takes time to change the identities and roles of women and men. It may also be the case that the desire to recognize the value of the personal sphere may act against the need to recruit women into the public sphere, where most political action takes place. Considering the political agenda of the women's movement, the idea that the personal is the political has had contradictory results. It has devalued the public sphere as violent and depersonalized (which it is), and it has often given people the mistaken impression that they can make significant political contributions by tending to their own gardens. The women's movement tried to break down the old split between the private and the public, but it has often ended by maintaining a strong sense of their boundaries because it has encouraged people to withdraw from the dangerous public sphere and to seek more privacy, and to celebrate interests and pursuits that cannot easily be shared with other human beings. Feminism has not only enlarged our definition of the political by incorporating the personal; it has contributed to the privatization of the public sphere. In this sense, the women's movement represents the finest flower of liberal individualism.

The debate over abortion rights reveals some of the problems created by the privatization of public life. Catharine MacKinnon has made the case that the shielding of abortions rights under the right to privacy has undermined the political power of women. According to her, the liberal court that ruled on *Roe v. Wade* as well as feminist defenders of abortion reaffirm and reinforce the split between public and private life because they define abortion as a personal choice and not as a public right. The right to have an abortion shares the same history in this argument with the right to have sex; choice is denied political weight, segregated in a private world, and protected only as part of the freedom of sexual expression. According to MacKinnon, the classification of choice under the right to privacy has had at least two major consequences. First, the Supreme Court could rule in *Harris v. McRae* that the right to abortion does not mean that funding by the federal government of medically necessary abortions is mandatory because the greatest concern of *Roe* was to guarantee "a woman's *decision* whether or not to terminate her pregnancy" (MacKinnon 1992, 355). Second, women have not been able to organize themselves politically on choice because the privacy issue makes it difficult to frame abortion rights according to a political agenda. In the final analysis, women have been unable to win a right uniquely important to them because it has been defined in terms of the private sphere and not in terms of public rights.

Sexual intercourse is not a personal act but an interpersonal one—that is, a social and political institution. Sexual politics stresses the political nature of all intercourse, sexual and otherwise, and attempts to frame intercourse in public terms. We should therefore understand that abortion rights cannot be protected under the right to privacy without also protecting criminal actions closely associated with the social institution of intercourse. Ironically, as MacKinnon explains, the same right to privacy that the courts use to protect abortion rights is extended to pornography, sexual battery, and marital rape. The privatization of women's lives is a form of oppression. I do not agree with MacKinnon that the distinction between public and private spheres is itself responsible for this oppression. It has been only a vehicle for it. But I agree with MacKinnon's description of the power politics that define the private and public spheres: "This right to privacy is a right of men 'to be let alone' to oppress women one at a time.... It keeps some men out of the bedrooms of other men" (MacKinnon 1992, 361–62).

The definition of women's politics as personal was perhaps inevitable, given the traditional view of women as private property. It may be true that defining the personal as political won rewards for women's self-esteem by giving value to their lives such as they existed, and this self-esteem may have been a necessary first ingredient for building political coalitions among women. But privatization also insulated women's concerns from the true locus of power and acted against coalition by separating women from each other. The reframing of *Roe v. Wade* by *Harris v. McRae* bears the strains of this privatization as much as it shows the imbalance of power between men and women, for although women were guaranteed the personal right to abortion by *Roe*, the right did not have to be recognized in the public sphere by the government. *Harris v. McRae* enabled the federal government to take a hands-off approach to abortion rights rather than to act aggressively to ensure them. Imagine if a similar situation evolved concerning the right to legal representation, which is a public right under the law. It would mean that an accused individual who could not afford legal representation could be put on trial without having a lawyer. The government would feel no obligation to provide legal representation or counsel.

Harris v. McRae confirms the need to redefine feminist politics according to the public sphere. It shows that the decision to retract the political into the private sphere in the early years of the women's movement now needs to be counteracted by the decision to introduce what is unique and different about women's concerns into the public sphere. There they will be subject to regulation by political debate, and, obviously, given the enormous bias against women in the political realm, it is imperative that they be able to participate in this debate, which means that women must run for public office, find ways of representing their views, create political-action groups to exert pressure, and demand that their perspectives be included in the law.

Gay and lesbian rights, it is worth noting briefly, raise similar issues. What is needed in the case of gay and lesbian rights is not less government in the bedroom but more government—but the right kind of government, by which I mean the same kind of law used to regulate heterosexual relationships. The right to register personal relationships in the public sphere protects their privacy and brings to them the benefits of many institutions and services, such as laws concerning inheritance, property rights, divorce, and medical and insurance benefits. Homosexual marriage and divorce need to be recognized under existing laws, so that all people, whatever their sexual orientation, have the choice whether to make public their sexual relationships and to submit them to the examination and protection of law.

The ethical imperative to ignore differences between people in favor of patterns of repetition rests at the heart of the politics of liberal democracy, and most of its laws and rights were created with this imperative in mind. Democratic society tends to view laws and rights as just only when they are defined universally, as equally applicable, without exception, to all members of the community. The new sexual

Introduction

politics, however, requires that we rethink the nature of our laws and rights with a mind to recognize not only the interpersonal and political dimension of human relationships but the important differences of individuals in our communities. Sexual politics suggests that liberal democracy may also determine its laws and rights according to an appreciation of the unique characteristics possessed by significant numbers of people living within it. Sexual difference is one such characteristic. The fact of sexuality demands that we create a new conception of laws and rights, one that will permit us to have our differences recognized in the public sphere without being made to suffer for them.

Retelling and Rereading

Narrative, in its minimal definition, happens when someone tells someone something and requires a retelling.[18] Rereading, whether it be an actual rereading or an interpretation of a reading, signals the presence of the narrative moment in the literary context. Narrative is a response to a happening that requires another response, and to respond, as Hannah Arendt understood, is both to give answer and to give account, which means that stories need to be interesting to survive (1955, 96). No interest, no story. The great test of a story is its ability to attract other people who desire to become the next teller of the tale, so that the experience of the narrative cannot be separated from its passing from person to person (Siebers 1992, 7). "It has seldom been realized," Walter Benjamin wrote, "that the listener's naive relationship to the storyteller is controlled by his interest in retaining what he has been told. The cardinal point for the unaffected listener is to assure

---

18. I am here modifying Barbara Herrnstein Smith's definition of narrative—"someone telling someone else that something happened" (1981, 228)—and Karl Kroeber's modification of Smith—"someone telling somebody something evoking evaluative responses" (1992, 229n1). Kroeber realizes that Smith needs to include an addressee's "interest" in her definition of narrative. "Evaluative response," however, may be too strong a label for this interest because retelling a story defines minimally a judgment or evaluation as well as captures the communal dimension of repetition. Kroeber insists on the singular importance of repetition for the definition of narrative many times (1, 55, 59, 177), making his work one of the strongest contributions to narrative theory in recent years. Paul Ricoeur's remarks on repetition have also been influential. He points to "narrative repetition" as a way to establish human action at the level of historicality, recommending it as an alternative to the dechronological approach of structuralist narratology (1981, 180). Narrative repetition has two other virtues: it is a form of recollection, and it possesses a communal dimension, since there is, for Ricoeur, no private narrative (183–84).

himself of the possibility of reproducing the story" (1968, 97). The interest in narrative is a form of being in human intercourse. This is why, Karl Kroeber explains, "stories improve with retelling, are endlessly retold, and are *told in order to be retold*" (1). The more often we hear a story and the more people who share it with us, the more the story is appreciated because it places us in a community of storytelling. Narrative interest creates an "in-between" that establishes both the role of the individual as a link in a chain of cultural conversations and the relation of narrative to all other forms of discourse—to verbal, symbolic, and social behavior in general. Notice, however, one anomaly in my definition of narrative: while these features may define narrative, they do not in extreme cases help to distinguish it from other forms of discourse because the most mundane utterance may well reproduce all of them. This fact does not threaten the definition of narrative but turns our attention to its defining characteristic and its greatest strength. Narrative does not need to escape mundanity to survive. It thrives on the mundane and worldly character of human intercourse. To survive, narrative needs only to be reproduced and repeated.

Ethics, aesthetics, and politics are particular modes of representing the repetition of experience, which is to say that they are modes of narrative discourse, and narrative in its minimal definition contains the stirrings of each mode. An ethical impulse grows in the requirement to repeat a story; this requirement is ethical in its lack of originality, its disgust for the differences needed for decision making, and its nonjudgmental embrace of another person's story. Aesthetics, too, may be recognized in the perception of the story form itself—that which must be repeated; aesthetics transcends repetition by giving it a pleasing form. In aesthetics we see that *something* counts and that it may be recounted. Politics emerges in the community created by the desire to put one's life into another person's story. The interest is in a life held in common, and it creates a solidarity that forges the chain of storytellers into a community. This community not only brings characters to life and offers them as guides for people's conduct. It serves as a community as such, which is to say that the aesthetics of storytelling always gives birth to an elementary form of politics (Siebers 1992, 81). When a story is told, heard, and retold, it creates an aesthetic community—an imaginary republic of citizens—that can be realized on the strength of the desire for community inspired by its very imagination. To imagine that something happened and to repeat it in imagination gives birth to a story, and only if we have the interest to tell and to retell a story will we be able to tell it well. From the

Introduction

goodness of retelling the story well emerges the form of the good held in common by ethics, aesthetics, and politics.

Another way to express this goodness is to view it as a form of nontrivial thinking or intelligence. Cornelius Castoriadis has made an argument for the importance of "the imaginary institution of society" in which creative imagination emerges as a core component of nontrivial thinking: "Whatever has been imagined strongly enough to shape behavior, speech or objects can, in principle, be reimagined (rerepresented, *wiedervorgestellt*) by somebody else" (1991, 85). According to Castoriadis, it is because social history is creative that the question of judging and choosing—in short, freedom—arises as a "radical, nontrivial question" (87). Every interpretation presupposes something that is not interpretable because every interpretation has an interest that may be interpreted by another interest. In other words, individuals reimagine other people's imaginings for their own ends. What cannot be denied, however, is that these private ends have a limit because interpreters wish to synthesize as many ends as possible; while interpretation creates both facts and communities, it is more concerned to create the communities in which facts have meaning than the facts themselves. Interpretations are bound by the need to be communicable, and the truth of facts will always give way, sooner or later, to the demand for community. A trend in continental philosophy, most identifiable with deconstruction, has often seen the self-refutability of argument as a threat to meaning and political formations. But self-refutation has no general consequences other than to make us aware that interpretation is the human activity par excellence. Even though they may appear as limits to interpretation, ethics, aesthetics, and politics cannot exist without interpretive freedom, and their interpretation is interminable. In it consists the nontrivial character of thinking.

Roger Schank, working in the entirely different field of artificial intelligence, has defined the goodness of storytelling as "intelligence." He has discovered that people judge the intelligence of computers in conversation with them on the basis of the ability to repeat stories. He calls this form of intelligence "reminding." Reminding is the ability both to repeat simple phrases and stories and to tell stories that seem to relate to other stories. "To the extent that intelligence," Schank claims, "is bound up with the ability to tell the right story at the right time, understanding a story means being able to correlate the story we are hearing with one that we already know. . . . Thus, seen this way, conversations are really a series of remindings" (1990, 21, 24).

At first glance, the idea of reminding appears to be an odd choice to define intelligence. We tend to associate intelligence with originality—thanks to romantic myths—and not with memory. But Schank's research exposes the fact that intelligence demands a strong awareness of the world in which invention occurs as well as an understanding of the effects that our inventions have on other people. The successful creation of different ideas requires that differences allude to a familiar context, that they be interesting and communicable to other persons, and that they be largely nonthreatening to existing social relationships. Intelligence is bound by the different imperatives of ethics, aesthetics, and politics, and whenever thought strays too far into one domain, it is pulled back by forces in the other domains, the objective being to make the greatest communication between people possible. The push and pull of creative thought are not always balanced, of course, and ideas are born that disturb individuals and disrupt communities. That we recognize the tension in intelligent thought between originality and memory, however, should demonstrate that creative modes such as ethics, aesthetics, and politics are always engaged in a tenuous dance with repetition. It also points to the fact that ethics is the dominant mode among the three, since its epic dream of the ultimate inclusive community motivates the desire to inscribe differences as much as possible within the spheres of memory and repetition.

We learn, if we learn at all—this is for history and the end of the time to know—by reexperiencing what has happened, for in the repetition of experience is born the concept of experience as such. Experience and its concept, however, require a story, and so different stories are told and retold. The heroes of tragedy learn by remembering and reexperiencing happenings that occur in what Hannah Arendt calls "the way of suffering" (1955, 20–21). By resuffering the past, they transform personal actions and experiences into public events in which we may recognize each other and the world. Even mundane events may become worldly if they are experienced a second time by memory in the form of tragic suffering, for then these events stir us to just anger, resentment, or stupefying indifference. The heroes of comedy, I want to claim, grow wise in their astonishment that their fall was fortunate, but they know happiness only because they fall more than once on the same spot. Their laughter and ours reconcile us to our inability to master our lives, saving us from that ambition with the happy conclusion that the world is a gentle place. Far less pleasurable is the nausea of repeating an experience with no sense of an end. When we are lucky, the repetition of narrative meets the repetition of experience as a homeopathic cure for nausea. Then the loathsome repetition comes abruptly and momentarily to an end, and one more *thing*, a story, graces the world.

2

What Does Postmodernism Want? Utopia

We conceive of our age as existing beyond the normal frames of time and space. Time flies, and yet each instant is crammed with things to do. Time-saving devices create more time but also require us to save more of it. Vast distances are crossed in no time at all, and yet we seem to spend all of our time either going from place to place or watching the world go by. There is no time to do nothing and no place to do it because doing nothing seems too much like doing something else.

Surely, this perception of time and space has to do with rapid advances in knowledge and technology, but it also reflects a transformation in the discourse of human desire. We hunger for change, self-transformation, and greater speed in transportation and information. We want to do what we have to do as fast as we can do it, so that we will have the pleasure of remembering it. This desire appears in the names that we give to ourselves. Our age has been called the "postindividual," the "posthistorical," the "postindustrial," even the "postcultural." We belong to a generation of followers, although we remain uncertain about what came before us or what might happen during our so-called postexistence. We live in a world without end, a world of infinite repetition, caught in the contradiction of both desiring an end and fearing it.

Postmodernism is the term used currently to bind together these perceptions, while the transformation of human desire is exposed in the repeated and urgent posing of the question, "What is postmodernism?" It is a question that no one has yet grown tired of asking, perhaps because it is, precisely, a question of desire.

Of course, to define postmodernism, we must know something about modernism—about what came before postmodernism and lies imbricated in it.[1] To understand modernism, however, we must

---

1. Andreas Huyssen (1986) provides to my mind the most judicious account of the modernist tendencies within postmodernism. I do think, however, that his idea

understand romanticism, the Enlightenment, the Renaissance, the Middle Ages, and so forth. Fortunately, given the daunting nature of this task, postmodernism rejects chronological thinking; it has little fondness for the grand narratives that might allow us to speak about the spirit of our age in a definite way. This does not mean, however, that we are off the hook as far as defining postmodernism is concerned. There would not be so many attempts today to define postmodernism, if definition were not a strong temptation. Nor would we be trying to define postmodernism, apparently, if we were really postmodern. There is something about postmodernism that creates a gap between saying what it is and trying to be it—which reveals once more that postmodernism turns on questions of desire.

All of this suggests that it may be difficult to be postmodern. In the spirit of this difficulty, I will not ask the question on everyone's lips, "What is postmodernism?" I will ask: "What does postmodernism want?" I am pastiching Freud's famous question about women, "Was will das Weib?"—but postmodernists like pastiche, so I hope that my question suits the times. More important, I am asking a question about desire—the desire of postmodernism—and like Freud's question, mine recognizes that I have little chance of finding an answer. Freud, a man, asked a question about woman's desire, thereby trying to understand a form of otherness—one probably created by asking the question in the first place. His question was both an earnest question and a sign of frustration—"*What* does woman want?" "What *does* woman want?"—and it takes its distance from woman's desire by asking about it. My question also has to look at postmodernism from a distance in order to frame its inquiry, and it expresses frustration, too.

But back to desire—which has something to do with earnest inquiry and frustration—back to want, which is what is desired and what is lacking. What postmodernism wants is what has been lacking, which is to say that postmodernism is a utopian philosophy. Utopianism demonstrates both a relentless dissatisfaction with the here and now as well as a bewilderment about the possibility of thinking beyond the here and now. Utopianism is not about being "nowhere"; it is about desiring to be elsewhere. This fact means that utopian desire has both hopeful and pessimistic sides: it yearns for happiness but only because it is so unhappy with the existing world. And if this

---

that modernism segregates high art from popular art applies more to modernist theory than to modern art. Consider, for example, the first modernist collage, Picasso's *Still Life with Chair Caning* (1912), which included an imitation cane design taken from a café tablecloth.

is true, attempts to distinguish between utopian and dystopian thinking are ultimately bound to fail. Utopian desire is the desire to desire differently, which includes the desire to abandon such desire.

Postmodernists, then, are utopian not because they do not know what they want. They are utopian because they know that they want something else. They want to desire differently. Of course, some factions within postmodernism have contempt for such desires, but is not this contempt merely another way of expressing the same old utopian desire to desire differently? It is no accident that the idea of utopia has emerged in the work of Donna Haraway, Fredric Jameson, and many others as the high concept of postmodernism. For postmodernism, like all utopian thinking, is concerned with what lies beyond the present moment, perhaps beyond any present moment.

My purpose here will be to discuss what postmodernism wants relative to three areas: cold-war politics, politics proper—by which I mean the romance of community—and aesthetics. In a sense, I will be trying to trace the historical and conceptual conditions unique to the postmodern desire for utopia, although obviously a full analysis lies beyond my powers here. The distinctive characteristics of postmodernism, I will argue, emerge partly in response to important concerns in these three areas, and its discourse of desire also emerges from what is wanting in these areas.

Post/War/Modernism

I know the danger in periodizing: there has never been a movement or period designation that has not shown some signs of emergence before it came into prominence. I nevertheless want to claim that a strong case exists for viewing postmodernism as a postwar phenomenon, whatever the various arguments about the historical emergence of the movement. The "post" in postmodernism displays an anxious awareness of the "post" in postwar, and we will never understand the prefix and its associations until we realize that they convey the emotional trauma of two world wars.[2]

If modernity expresses the desire to capture a sense of wholeness, of the end of destiny pictured in single aesthetic objects, be they *Finnegans Wake* or a Brancusi sculpture, then the very concept of world war is modernist.[3] It is in response to this concept that post-

---

2. For a more detailed argument, see Siebers 1993, chaps. 2 and 7.

3. The reader will notice that I use *modernity* and *modernism* interchangeably. This is because the desire for self-legitimacy ascribed to modernity in its now-classic

modernism will define itself. The concept is, of course, highly metaphorical, but then we live in a world that privileges figurative meaning above all others, and this preference is central to how postmodernists conceive of their difference from other movements and times. Whether unified positively in the United Nations or unified negatively in world war, modernism is seen as having a predisposition toward homogeneity.[4] *Finnegans Wake* demonstrates a wholeness by virtue of the opaqueness of its style and the gluttony of its reference, and Brancusi's sculptures are viewable in the wink of an eye. T. S. Eliot's idea of tradition and individual talent is also modernist because he conceived of individual talent as crystallizing retrospectively in its very form the entire direction of past tradition. Technological mod-

---

definition cannot be represented without using the modernist concept of aesthetic autonomy. Modernity is rarely at war with modernism, therefore, while modernism, as the privileged vehicle of modernity's self-representation, always struggles and fails to free itself from the secular and political project of modernity, the paradoxical result being that modern art subordinates the human world and its stories to a nonrepresentational and nonnarrative picture of the world, in short, to a landscape devoid of human forms.

What distinguishes postmodernism, I will be arguing, is not the desire to homogenize differences, *pace* modernity, but the desire to put together things that do not belong together. The desire for heterogeneity, which may be said to be desire at its most exacerbated, characterizes the aesthetic and political ambitions of postmodernism, but its political ambitions, as in the case of modernity, must be represented aesthetically, which is why I devote the section below to the study of Jackie Winsor's sculpture.

4. The spectacle of the world coming together is what modernity envisions in one form or another; what it eventually gets is the world falling apart. Its founding myth, which lies behind both its obsessional constructivism and its fascination with analytic dissection, is that a big picture does exist and that its story can be told. But modernity becomes increasingly disenchanted with the desire for wholeness after the experience of World War I, and by the end of World War II, it rejects narratives about world community outright as one of the most dangerous forms of myth, frequently to the point of seeing any form of narrative as corrupt.

Certain elements of postmodernism shun narrative for the same reason, but they are more easily identified with postmodern theory than with its art forms. This is why many so-called postmodernists, who started out as poststructuralists, are finally not very postmodern. Jean-François Lyotard, for example, defines postmodernism in opposition to modernity and its desire to invent grand narratives. Very quickly, however, his distaste for grand narrative spreads to all narratives. There is no room for storytelling in Lyotard's theories because sooner or later every story is seen as serving one interest and as trying to give that interest dominance over all others. For Lyotard, stories are the lies that we tell to others in order to have our way with them.

On the modern loss of faith in utopian narratives, see Hughes 1980, chap. 4. See also Lyotard 1984.

ernization, too, belongs to modernity in its drive toward efficiency and completeness. It wants to polish the world to a bright gleam as if it were an apple.

Of course, one can find many countertrends in modernism: primitivism, assemblage, and so forth. My point is only that postmodernists see a political danger associated with the modern and that it is of a certain kind, one best described as having to do with the global nature of politics conceived during the years of the world wars and cold war. The enemy twins of modernity—capitalism and communism—were false twins in many ways, but they were true twins in their mutual hatred and in the manner in which each compacted the world in a defensive posture against the other. Each one in some way envisioned its art, literature, crafts, architecture, political forms, and quotidian activities as expressing a unique and singular vernacular. Each one viewed itself as a complete picture of how the world should be, but neither one knew how to include the other in this world. The dream that everything should be of a piece sweetened the sleep of modernity and united its politics and aesthetics. Both capitalist modernization and communist vanguardism were lulled by this dream.

Today this dream has become our worst political nightmare. Postmodernism tries to present a counterspirit to this political danger, but, of course, it is not always successful or at all certain that it wants to be a counterspirit. Debates about whether postmodernism is democratic or totalitarian, liberal or conservative, are therefore retrograde, although perhaps necessary to any truly political conception of the world.[5] These arguments miss the fundamental orientation of postmodernism, which is to escape from concepts as logically monolithic as the "political." If everything is political, if everything, that is, could belong to a single logic called the political, then this fact alone would be reason enough to war against its totality, although it is not clear that a true postmodernist would be able to sustain the conviction necessary to the battle.

Postmodernism wants to displace our attention from the logic of forms to their variety, from wholes to parts. Its interest in technology is geared toward recovery of lost forms and their reproduction in pastiche, playful citation, and collecting. Postmodernism has a scrapbook attitude toward the past, eagerly borrowing from it but assem-

---

5. These questions are fundamental because it is politically important to choose between democracy and totalitarianism, but this act of choice flies in the face of a certain postmodern reading of what choice is. Politics always looks somewhat retrograde from the postmodern vantage point; but, then, from a political angle, postmodernism looks very silly.

bling the pieces in new patterns. Perhaps one sees this aesthetic attitude best expressed in postmodern architecture, where borrowings create softer edges than those found in modernist buildings. Postmodernism has a distinctive hatred of dualisms and binary oppositions, the greatest one of the twentieth century being democracy versus totalitarianism. Postmodernists want to do away with the Truman Doctrine in politics and aesthetics by putting together things that do not belong together. The trend toward multiculturalism is therefore one of the most popular and best signs of the influence of the postmodern ethic. It is at once a utopian dream about a harmonious planet and a dream about wholeness in which various parts are allowed their autonomy. More important, multiculturalism sees the Third World as a resource for thinking our way out of the frightening dualities and impasses of the postwar era.

To use the language of their political philosophy, postmodernists want to preserve a sense of "concrete otherness" within models of equality rather than to focus on similarity (see Benhabib 1992, chap. 5). Suffice it to say that a fundamental trait of postmodernism is its belief that equality is healthy; otherwise, postmodernists would not be so eager to describe equality in terms of difference. For them, equality is always the product not of sameness but of differences, and they are confident that all differences are equal. I do not think that this confidence can be thought of in any other way except as a historical perception of the postwar world. Let me be very clear: postmodernism is the recipient of the modern drive toward a homogeneous world, but in the failure of the modernist drive, the breaking of the world into two halves—capitalist and communist—postmodernism sees a failure of both vision and ambition because modernity not only created a world of total conflict but failed to include a great deal that could not be defined in terms of the superpower duality of the postwar world. Despite massive efforts, the twin political ideologies of modernity could not prevent their vision of the whole from falling apart.

This failure is for postmodernists the best proof that heterogeneity and multiplicity are irrepressible. When postmodernists take a positive view of this legacy and celebrate difference, their political gestures and art forms are almost giddy. Their sense of confidence in a new world overwhelms their means of expression, producing bizarre and sometimes goofy conglomerations of ideas and objects.[6] The giddiness of postmodernism, however, sometimes turns into nausea, and

---

6. Huyssen (1986) describes postmodernism as initially "future happy" and traces how it loses its confidence.

then postmodern collage descends into monstrosity and pollution, taking an almost masochistic pleasure in its ability to cannibalize even the most disparate ideas and forms. What postmodernism tries to do in both cases, however, is to create a picture with emphasis on all the parts, to avoid conflictual dualism, and to collect and to combine as much as possible into a new vision. This desire defines both the politics and aesthetics of postmodernism.

Perhaps postmodernism is a grand narrative after all, although one based on the rejection of grand narratives—a grand narrative in spite of itself, then, and what could be more difficult than that?

The Romance of Community

Another but related way of envisioning the utopian desire of postmodernism—for remember we are talking not about what postmodernism has done but about what it wants—is to broach the topic of the romance of community. We imagine our communities through symbols. These symbols take the form of buildings, monuments, and public spaces, but they can be as exotic as works of art or as mundane as the shapes of automobiles, toasters, patio furniture, and shoes. The aesthetic sensibility of any movement registers desires about its politics. Its forms are in part forms of politics.

The best place to discuss forms of community in postmodernism is to analyze its symbolic relationship to feminism because this relationship is a romance. I confess that I had this direction in mind when I borrowed Freud's famous question about woman's desire. Even though it has taken some time for feminists to become interested in postmodernism—an indifference now thoroughly reversed—questions about sexuality and gender lie at its heart. The emergence and symbolic character of this romance can be again conceived historically.[7] Classicism is patriarchal in its desire to define social forms as passing from father to son. The model in government is monarchical. This system endures more or less until the Enlightenment, when fraternity replaces the patriarchal model. Here equality evolves for the first time as a popular movement, but it is conceived in terms of universal brotherhood. That is to say, it is an affair among men. With the rise of romanticism, however, something begins to happen to the parliamentary model of rule by brotherhood. *Love* replaces *brotherhood* in the language of equality, and slowly but surely sexual difference begins to

---

7. I take elements of the following schema from MacCannell 1991.

be felt. The sexual body also becomes the metaphor for the body politic, and it acquires a power of symbolization formerly reserved for public spaces, buildings, and monuments. By the nineteenth century, in fact, utopian communities were being founded out of the desire for sexual as much as for political happiness. These developments, of course, issued from a very long and drawn-out process, and we are still experiencing the evolution today. My point, however, is that the new model of community is based on the romantic couple.

The metaphor of the couple is one of the grand themes passed from romanticism to modernism and postmodernism. With postmodernism it has generated concrete applications in terms of the rights of women, and one cannot conceive of postmodernism without giving sexual happiness its due. The postmodern romance of community is based on the idea of sexual difference. It gives us one of the best visions of equality, one based on difference rather than sameness. I do not think that it is an accident that the burning ethical and political issues of our day have to do with sexuality and reproductive technologies: abortion rights, artificial insemination, test-tube babies, sex change, sterilization, cosmetic surgery, family values, date rape, and the gay military. Nor is it an accident that male politicians are declining to run for second terms because they want to spend more time with their families. We now conceive of utopia according to sexual politics.

For these reasons and others, it is to be expected that postmodern attempts to define utopia will relate it in some connection to sexual happiness and the body political. Judith Shklar (1994) provides some useful background to this development. She suggests that the classical utopia, which is based on purely civic values, repairs to its deathbed in the work of Rousseau, whose pessimism, solipsism, and emphasis on sexual passion begin to shatter the homogeneity of the traditional model. Even though Rousseau views humankind as naturally good, its goodness, for him, can be divined only in the solitary individual, the result being that collective efforts are doomed to failure. Whenever two individuals come together to live—and inevitably in Rousseau these individuals are a man and a woman—their passions and sense of obligation ruin their society. Rousseau was among the first to view society in terms of the properties of the sexual couple, but his judgment of its potential for creating happiness was negative and misogynist. He blamed the decline of culture on the feminization of society, and all of his models of successful utopias were unreservedly masculinist. Incidentally, the various American utopian communities that sprang up in the nineteenth century (among them Fourier's phalanxes and Noyes's Oneida) were in part a response to Rousseau's beliefs. These communities accepted his romantic definition of culture, including its emphasis on sexual politics, and so they resolved to mend the ills of social existence by trying to reduce first and foremost sexual conflicts and unhappiness.

By the 1960s, according to Shklar, *politics* no longer refers to public practices of self-government among people who freely choose to live in common, and political science is beginning to succumb to sexual politics and family planning. She makes a point of attacking the communal living experiments of the 1960s as apolitical: they were not, she argues, true political attempts to transform humanity but experiments with alternative families. In fact, however, alternative family living could, and did, lay claim to being the most recognizable and valuable form of political experimentation. Alternative families and free love were the means by which people were going to transform humanity and to save themselves from their own violence, if, in fact, it was possible. Indeed, Steven Seidman (1992) has argued that sexual politics has completely taken over the definition of the political in postwar America.

The community of postmodernism has become the family unit, broadly defined, because it is one of the most nonexclusionary models available for community and it has all the right emotions—love and acceptance. Therefore, it is ironic but predictable that "family values" would become the explicit theme of our times: ironic, because it has become a theme in a compromised way, since the current proponents of family values try to turn the family again into an exclusionary term; predictable, because we are all actively trying to make our political communities match the politics of the romantic couple. Gay and lesbian rights have emerged as an issue with such tremendous force because they represent the last frontier in the definition of the couple: sexual politics defines the couple as the site of difference, but the concept of the couple will not be wholly inclusive until we are able to accept the nondifference of same-sex partners within its definition. Once gays and lesbians are allowed to pair off, without exciting accusations of deviancy, the model of community based on the couple will be entirely nonexclusionary. Everyone will have an equal opportunity to be happy.

It is a pity, however, that the community founded on the romance of the couple may be most threatened by the pressures of the economic world that it has created; as partners gain equal access to society and work, the ideal of the romantic couple is being replaced by that of the "working couple." Community is losing its "romance," as people struggle to find time to be together. The family is disappearing even as we fight to broaden its definition and to ensure its survival. What postmodernism wants most, it finds in tatters about it.

Postmodern Aesthetics

Objects of art, like romances of community, are allegories of desire, and postmodern art is explicitly utopian in its desire. There are two major properties of postmodern art: a love of narrative and a desire to assemble. They are related. The desire to assemble is, of course, as much a metaphor for community as for aesthetic creation. Postmodernism creates its idea of utopia by affirming the desire to bring things together and by insisting that the story of the assembly be told. Indeed, many postmodern works lose their meaning unless one knows the story behind them. This is why they rely so heavily on citation. Unlike modernist art, which actively excludes narrative from its aesthetics, postmodern art wants its audience to hear the story behind the object and works hard to tell it.

The work of the postminimalist sculptress Jackie Winsor, who in 1979 was the youngest artist ever and the first woman to have a retrospective at the Museum of Modern Art in New York, conveys something of the flavor of postmodern aesthetics and its obsession with assembly and storytelling. Winsor moves beyond the minimalist trends of modernism by adding natural materials to industrial ones and by creating sculptures with human volume and scale. She uses basic elements of composition in her sculpture—rope, wire, concrete, and wood—rather than piecing together ready-made or found objects. Her vocabulary of forms remains modernist in the choice of basic shapes, such as the cube or the sphere, but in her hands they acquire a texture and meaningfulness not always found in modernist sculpture. Her objects do not strive for Platonic universals, as in modernism, but realize particular forms of the cube or the sphere that are both perfect and flawed in their thingness. Winsor's sculptures are handworked, charged with the ritual drama of their making, and display an obsessive sense of repetition: her pieces show signs of repeated wrapping, nailing, and painting, and it clearly requires muscle to make them. She also uses braiding and knotting, thereby incorporating into her art crafts associated with women.

Most important, Winsor's work is explicitly about assembly: "What my work is about is putting things together and putting things together a lot. I'm interested in what is holding things together and in presenting you with the real, in a real way so you get to read what that realness is about" (Gruen 1979, 59). Every one of her objects is made through a meticulous, difficult, and time-consuming process, where each laying on of her hands is recorded in the artwork and dwelt upon self-consciously by the artist herself, as if the sculpture involved an act of self-creation and self-maturation. "They're kind of slow pieces," Winsor says of her sculptures, "quiet, self-contained. They're a way of stilling something, absorbing all momentary states of being and giving them a common denominator, like someone old, who's put in a lot of months and years" (Glueck 1979, C20).

The goal of Winsor's art is not only the creation of an object but the savoring of the work and rhythms that go into its creation. Either she uses materials that already have meaning for her or she invents a "studio ceremony," a process of assembly, that charges her materials with personal meaning (Winsor 1972, 13). In both cases, this meaning is conveyed most fully only by seeing the sculpture and learning the story of its assembly at the same time.

Green Piece, for example, reworks the modernist cube, but its materials are more particular, more personal, and it openly exhibits the signs of its making (fig. 1). It is a methodically crafted piece, with no signs of manufacturing, and its size bestows upon the work a human aura. The cool, green surface of antique wainscoting gives the piece a homey feeling and a sense of having endured for a long time, and yet the object is not all surface because five windows allow the viewer to peer into its interior spaces. The windows seize the viewer's curiosity and give an added dimension to the piece: it cannot be grasped in the single wink of an eye, and it tempts the viewer to walk around it, to stoop down, to hunch over it, and perhaps to reach inside.

Green Piece is too early for Winsor to be making a pun on *green peace*, but it does gather associations of the earthly globe, and it possesses an inherent ecology, because Winsor constructed the piece out of recycled materials taken from her studio walls. The homey quality of the sculpture is not merely formal, therefore; it springs from Winsor's own mental image of the materials and their history. Once upon a time, this old green wainscoting covered the interior of her studio, providing an aura of familiarity and comfort. Then Winsor turned her studio inside out, creating a little room, an *atelier de l'artiste*, whose exterior was once an interior and whose new interior conveys the feelings of concentration, memory, and mysterious creation previously found within the walls of her studio.

Painted Piece (fig. 2) resembles *Green Piece* in its form and volume, but its concept is different. Winsor created its personality

Fig. 1. Jackie Winsor, *Green Piece*, 1976–77. Painted wood, cement, nails. 32½″ × 32½″ × 32½″. Modern Art Museum of Fort Worth, Texas. (Photograph by Geoffrey Clements.)

through a combination of studio ceremony and chance. She applied fifty layers of paint to its exterior and interior, alternating coats of pink, red, blue-gray, black, and goldenrod, before adding a finish of dark gray. Winsor mapped her progress by making a swatch of each color on a sheet of paper before applying the coat, creating a record of the work's topography.[8] Then she chained the piece to the back of her car and dragged it down Mercer to Broome on the sidewalk in front of her studio. To get extra contact, she sat on the cube but was dissatisfied with the effect, so that evening she brought in six friends for added weight. They took the cube across the street to the parking lot, sat on it, and dragged it around again (Tallmer 1982, 9). Her original idea was that the rough surface of the street would skin off the outer layers of paint, exposing in the scrapes and gouges an archaeology of color (Winsor 1986, 32). But the dragging produced an intense friction that heated and mixed the paint, creating unexpected fusions of color reminiscent of abstract expressionism.

Painted Piece reveals a clue to Winsor's art and to its postmodern ethic. Unlike the minimalism of modernist art, the process and ideals of her art are sometimes far apart and often deliberately so. "Minimalism is an intellectual formula," Winsor explains, "and my approach is more experiential" (Mifflin 1989, 90). The ritual of daily applications of paint habituates the artist to the object, making it familiar and charging it with personal associations and feelings of concern; then chance enters the picture, scorching the work and branding it with a peculiar identity. Care and chance combine to age the work and to give it a volume of experience that can be sensed by the viewer. They also extend and enrich the narrative of the object, making it into a souvenir of astonishing happenings and diverse emotions. The work exists not only for itself but as an occasion to tell a story.

Exploded Piece (fig. 3) carries Winsor's experiments with the work of care and chance even further. First, Winsor constructed a cube of plaster and reinforced concrete, finishing its exterior with a coat of gunmetal gray and decorating its interior plaster walls with a delicate gold-leaf paint. Then she hauled the eighteen-hundred-pound cube down two flights of stairs from her SoHo studio into a field on Long Island, where demolition experts from the film industry blew up the cube with plastic explosives under the supervision of the fire department. Winsor had built the cube to contain the explosion, but the demolition people used a high-intensity, low-impact rather than a low-intensity, high-impact explosive. Her intention had been to trau-

---

8. Sobel 1991 provides a photographic record of the daily ritual.

Fig. 2. Jackie Winsor, *Painted Piece*, 1979–80. Plywood, acrylic paint (50 layers). 31" × 31" × 31" (JW 41). Milwaukee Art Museum. (Photograph by Geoffrey Clements.)

matize the interior walls of the cube, but the explosion tore the whole piece asunder, reducing it to little more than rubble (fig. 4).[9]

Winsor had spent the summer assembling the cube, and it took a month for the paint to cure. Now she found herself face to face with the destruction of her work, and a sense of her own vulnerability engulfed her.[10] She gathered up the debris and restored the cube as best as she could to its original state. One cannot see the damage to the exterior of the piece, but its interior bears the marks of the accident. Explosive residues have penetrated the gold-leaf paint, and the plaster is cracked in some places and pulverized in others. The fractured state gives the interior surfaces the appearance of a ruined fresco or the walls of an ancient church. The overall effect is remarkable, turning on a contrast between the dark, sullen, cratelike appearance of the cube's exterior and its fragile contents. The experience of the work is akin to the revelation of peering through the doors of a soot-covered church to discover in the narrow beam of light a luminous interior of gilded frescoes, precious statuary, and ceremonial candlelight.

Exploded Piece shows form and force working together. It actively incorporates destruction into the process of construction, but its emphasis lies finally on construction. If *Green Piece* shows us the fragility of an environment and *Painted Piece* takes a certain enjoyment in destruction, then *Exploded Piece* demonstrates how the urge to destroy may get out of hand and that our need to try to put things together again is urgent. If we see these pieces as metaphors of the earth, they combine to tell the story of recent world history in which the earth had lost its preciousness and then regained it.

Conclusion

Winsor's cubes expose the fragility of the world and incorporate into art the debris and residues of our most violent desires. They tell the story of the desire to bring things together, without losing the sense of their individuality and vulnerability. They stress, moreover, that the love of this kind of storytelling may be necessary to sustain the ability to assemble, whether we are talking about objects of art or communities. Indeed, the political version of this form of assembly, a commu-

---

9. Winsor tells the story of *Exploded Piece* in Tallmer 1982.

10. "The unknown blew the whole thing apart, physically and emotionally. Because of that moment in the piece when it was blown apart and how big that moment felt to me I became aware of my own incredible vulnerability" (Winsor 1986, 32).

Fig. 3. Jackie Winsor, *Exploded Piece*, 1980–82. Wood, reinforced concrete, plaster, gold leaf, explosive residue 34½" × 34½" × 34½" (JW-43-SC). Private collection.

Fig. 4. Jackie Winsor, *Exploded Piece* (in progress), 1980–82. Wood, reinforced concrete, plaster, gold leaf, explosive residue. 34½″ × 34½″ × 34½″ (JW 43).

nity with many different stories, is embraced in one version or another throughout postmodernism; it represents the postmodern vision of utopia, where community is based on the inclusion of differences, where heterogeneity does not inspire conflict, and where different forms of talk are allowed to exist simultaneously.

The lesson of modernism is that one cannot unburden oneself of bad politics through the wholesale rejection of storytelling because narrative is a central element in all politics, perhaps more so in good than in bad.[11] Every form of politics has a kind of narrative style, an aesthetic taste, since the types of stories embraced and rejected by nations accumulate to create their founding mythologies and the visions upon which they build their futures. This is why "cultural politics," an idea that stresses both the aesthetics of political cultures and the politics of aesthetic cultures, is so central to the postmodern worldview. It is also why no argument about the utopian philosophy of postmodernism dares exclude an appraisal of its aesthetic taste. A story, as it is passed from imaginer to imaginer, as it is told, retold, and "told in order to be retold" (Kroeber 1992, 1), creates an aesthetic community—an imaginary republic of citizens—that rivals any worldly republic and that can be realized on the strength of the desire for community inspired by its very imagination.[12] It is not a pure community—one purified of conflicting interests—but a community with many different stories.

It is difficult in the end to quibble with what postmodernism wants, even though it is doubtful that we will ever have it. Postmodernism wants us to think the contradictions of human existence at the speed of light in order to find in the relativity of time a way to reconcile our differences; but these differences are not always so easily reconciled, and many questions linger. Inasmuch as they are questions about our desire, they remain utopian, suggesting that postmodernity is perhaps the most expansively utopian age of all.

---

11. The defining feature of modernism, Karl Kroeber (1992, 1) argues, is its rejection of storytelling. This expulsion should be seen in terms of modernism's disenchantment with utopian narratives.

12. See chap. 1. On self-imagining societies, see also Castoriadis 1991.

Multiculturalism, or the Ethics of Anti-Ethnocentrism

My goal in creating this collage is to assemble a variety of opinions, anecdotes, and arguments found at the crossroads where current debates about multiculturalism and ethnocentrism may be said to meet. My first presupposition is that the West is an "anthropological culture" in which self-image is constructed within the history of an ethnographic encounter with other cultures. This fact accounts for the disparity between the moral status of anthropology in the West and the feelings of moral hypochondria from which ethnographers often suffer. One version of Western morality, sometimes called cosmopolitanism, believes that encounters between cultures, if conducted in an anthropological spirit, will lead to the emergence of a harmonious world community. Many ethnographers in the field, however, are haunted by fears that their attempts to communicate with other cultures merely oppress them, and that attempts at communication serve a dubious and ethnocentric ethic, at best misguided and at worst colonialist.

My second presupposition is that current debates about multiculturalism retain the moral and political descriptions invented by this anthropological tradition but apply them to individual nations. *Multiculturalism* refers most often to internal conflicts within one nation, polity, or geographical enclave rather than to disputes between separate political or national cultures. In this country, it tries to place in question the traditional curriculum in order to represent fairly the variegated nature of American culture. It also demands that marginalized groups and minority peoples be empowered. Arguments about multiculturalism, however, frequently reproduce moral and political dilemmas first experienced by ethnographers, and the term itself owes its emergence and significance to the anthropological spirit of Western culture.

Two questions would seem to be paramount, if these presuppositions hold. (1) To what extent is the difference between anti-ethnocentrism and multiculturalism an expression of giving emphasis to intercultural over intracultural distinctions? Or, to rephrase, can a culture treat its differences from other cultures in the same way that it treats differences within itself? I submit that this question must lead to an attempt to understand the opposition between ethics and politics, since ethics strives for a wholly nonexclusive, atemporal community and politics works to design an inclusive, historical community. Whence the second master question of this chapter. (2) By their very terms are anti-ethnocentrism and multiculturalism tautological preferences for the ethical that deny the viability of the political as such? Or, to rephrase again, is the dream of the possibility of a nonexclusive community, formulated at the heart of anti-ethnocentrism and multiculturalism, an ethical vision that defines ethics as such in the action of isolating itself from politics? Incidentally, if the answer to this second question is yes, my title is a trap set for the cosmopolitan moralist—whom I reserve the right to exhibit, should I catch one.

Anti-Ethnocentrism

The Case of the Drunken Indian and the Kidney Machine

The extreme shortage, due to their great expense, of artificial kidney machines led, naturally enough, to the establishment a few years ago of a queuing process for access to them by patients needing dialysis in the government medical program in the southwestern United States directed, also naturally enough, by young, idealistic doctors from major medical schools, largely northeastern. . . . The Indian, after gaining access to the scarce machine refused, to the great consternation of the doctors, to stop, even to control, his drinking, which was prodigious. His position . . . was: I am indeed a drunken Indian, I have been one for quite some time, and I intend to go on being one as long as you can keep me alive by hooking me up to this damn machine of yours. The doctors . . . regarded the Indian as blocking access to the machine by others on the queue, in no less desperate straits, who could, as they saw it, make better use of its benefits—a young, middle-class type, say, rather like themselves. . . . As the Indian was already on the machine by the time the problem because visible they could not bring themselves (nor, I suppose, would they have been permitted) to take him off it; but they were very deeply upset—at least as upset as the Indian, who was disciplined enough to show up promptly for all his appointments, was resolute. (Geertz 1986, 115–16)

Geertz advances this story as a parable to understand the uses of diversity in modern life. It is no accident that it pictures an Indian, a former object of anthropological study, in confrontation with our Western anthropological culture. Only this time it is the Indian who has come to visit. Geertz's point is to discredit two recent defenses of anti-anti-ethnocentrism. Both Lévi-Strauss and Richard Rorty have worried that anti-ethnocentrism misapprehends the importance of ethnocentrism in maintaining cultural diversity. This diversity, Lévi-Strauss argues, "results from the desire of each culture to resist the cultures surrounding it, to distinguish itself from them—in short to be itself" (cited by Geertz 1986, 107). Rorty claims that postmodern bourgeois liberals—the natives of Western democracies—need to understand that loyalty to our society is loyalty enough, in short, that the West should be responsible only to its own traditions. Geertz fears that such attitudes will cultivate deafness, maximize "gratitude for not having been born a Vandal or an Ik," and make the world safe for condescension (110).

To these two versions of "to-each-his-own morality," Geertz opposes an anthropological ethic. Rather than seeing other cultures as alternatives *to* us, we should see them as alternatives *for* us: "The trouble with ethnocentrism is not that it commits us to our own commitments. We are, by definition, so committed, as we are to having our own headaches. The trouble with ethnocentrism is that it impedes us from discovering at what sort of angle . . . we stand to the world" (1986, 112).

I begin with Geertz on Rorty (and Lévi-Strauss) because he formulates two options inherent in the confrontation between different groups. We may see the other as the other, or we may see the other as material useful to change ourselves (Siebers 1992, 136–37). Although Geertz is interested in anthropology from the native's point of view, he prefers the second option. He wants to *use* diversity. But diversity is not what it used to be, as his parable demonstrates. The world, he complains, is smaller, and true strangeness and oddness are in short supply. The multiculture is becoming a monoculture. The future of ethnocentrism is therefore bound to change. As the world grows smaller, we may expect examples of ethnic diversity not to be isolated in remote jungles or on exotic islands but to be growing in our midst, whatever "our midst" comes to mean. This fact, Geertz explains, will require more imagination on our part, not the imagination to make up diversity but the imagination required to pick out subtle examples of it.

"The Drunken Indian and the Kidney Machine" provides a case in point. Geertz worries about the case because he sees so little understanding on either side, but he comes down, as we might expect, on the side of the drunken Indian. For Geertz believes that the doctors had little appreciation for the historical turmoil that made the Indian a drunk. Yet Geertz can offer no solution to the situation: "I cannot see that either more ethnocentrism, more relativism, or more neutrality would have made things any better (though more imagination might have)" (1986, 117). The episode takes place in the dark for Geertz because no one grasped what it was to be the other and no one learned much in the episode about either themselves or anyone else. In a sense, what everyone lacked was the point of view of the ethnographer. Ethnography, Geertz claims, "places particular we-s among particular they-s, and they-s among we-s, where all . . . already are, however uneasily" (119). It teaches us that we must know others and live with that knowledge, and it accomplishes this feat by making us visible to ourselves by representing us and everyone else "as cast into the midst of a world full of irremovable strangeness we can't keep clear of" (120). In the final analysis, the use of diversity is to make us understand that we live in a collage of otherness.

Rorty's response to Geertz is that anti-ethnocentrism is the particular ethnocentric bias of the West, which means that anti-anti-ethnocentrism should be viewed not as ethnocentric behavior but as a self-critical attitude on the part of pragmatists and postmodern bourgeois liberals. "We would rather die than be ethnocentric," he writes, "but ethnocentrism is precisely the conviction that one would rather die than share certain beliefs. We find ourselves wondering whether our own bourgeois liberalism is not just one more example of cultural bias" (Rorty 1986, 525).

The gist of Rorty's argument is best explained by looking at his reading of "The Drunken Indian and the Kidney Machine." He sees the darkness of the episode but believes that there was enough light for everyone to do what was required. There is no need for improvement. The drunken Indian had the right to be on the machine, and if the doctors has removed him for one of their own—which they did not—the authorities would have descended upon them. In short, procedural justice was served in the case, and to ask that the participants understand each other more or love each other more simply misunderstands how the political ethics of Western democracies works. The moral tasks of a liberal democracy, according to Rorty, are divided between the agents of love and the agents of justice. Agents of love and connoisseurs of diversity, such as anthropologists, insist that society notice people who are different, and they then make these people candidates for admission to society by explaining their odd behavior. The agents of justice make sure that "once these people are admitted as citizens, once they have been shepherded into the light by the connoisseurs of diversity, they are treated just like all the rest of us" (1986, 529). For Rorty, there is something unique and worth preserving about this kind of society. His form of pragmatism holds that Western ideals may be "local and culture-bound"—ethnocentric—"and nevertheless be the best hope for the species" (532).

Let me add, briefly, that the crux of my argument about the paradoxes of ethnocentrism is found in the dispute between Geertz and Rorty, and it goes something like this: a connoisseur of diversity, if he or she is really a connoisseur, will tend to be an aesthete, which means that diversity will become an end in itself. Diversity metamorphoses into an aesthetic object, and the connoisseur dwells on the oddness, uniqueness, and originality of that object, often claiming that only he or she truly understands its value. We may call it diversity for diversity's sake. Aestheticism is objectionable on the current scene because it both objectifies difference and lacks political motivation. Nevertheless, the moment that the connoisseur departs from aestheticism and tries to find a "use" for diversity, political or otherwise, he or she can be accused of "using" someone else for selfish purposes. Geertz, for example, believes in the uses of diversity, and this means that his use has a purpose. The purpose is to create a harmonious world culture, beginning with the enrichment and enlargement of the sensibilities of the Western population that he represents. In short, Geertz almost agrees with Rorty's ethnocentrism, but he is shy about stating his intentions.

Rorty, however, agrees less with Geertz than Geertz with him because Geertz smells of cosmopolitan morality. Geertz is too much the connoisseur, and his anti-ethnocentrism flows from an aesthetic sensibility. In Rorty's language, Geertz is trying to stand in too many places at the same time, to appreciate too much, and he ends up standing nowhere as a result. Anti-ethnocentrism, according to this argument, robs one of a political base.

To understand how Geertz gets into this position and why it is the case, I must sketch several distinct phases in the encounter between the anthropologist and the cultural other.

Tylor's Time Machine

> No doubt the life of the less civilized peoples of the world, the savages and barbarians, is more wild, rough and cruel than ours is on the whole, but the difference between us and them does not lie altogether in this. As the foregoing chapters have proved, savage and barbarous tribes often more or less fairly represent stages of culture through which our own ancestors passed long ago, and their customs and laws often explain to us in ways we should otherwise have hardly guessed, the sense and reason of our own. (Tylor, cited by McGrane 1989, 93)

In the earliest phases of modern anthropology, under the influence of Darwin, the difference between the ethnographer and native other was formulated as a matter of temporal or historical difference. Anthropology was, in McGrane's words, a time machine by which the West sought to voyage back in time to examine its own evolutionary progress. To leave Europe or the United States was to explore the past, and the diversity encountered by the ethnographer merely exposed various historical moments in the grand progression leading to his or her own age.

Me Anthropologist, You Native

> I must say here something of the qualities of the Anuak fighters. They are brave, but become very excited and expose themselves unnecessarily.... They must be led. They will go with you anywhere and will not desert you in a scrap if things go badly, but they will not go without you.... I learnt that if, after discussion of the course of action I proposed they refuse to agree to it, I could attain my object by proceeding to carry out the proposed operation myself, whereupon all eventually followed suit. (Evans-Pritchard, cited by Geertz 1985b, 54)

In this phase, the encounter between ethnographer and native provides the opportunity for the anthropologist to educate (to lead out of darkness) native others, thereby helping them to live up to their potential, a potential best exemplified by the ethnographer.

What is most striking about Evans-Pritchard's description of the Anuak, however, is not his own sense of superiority—although it is instructive, since it is the base from which cosmopolitan morality is launched—but the Anuak's preference for "solidarity" over "objectivity." These are Rorty's terms for the fundamental tension between epistemological and political moralities. We have a basic choice when deciding to act: we can support the truth or we can support our neighbor. To choose the first is to be objective; to choose the second is to support solidarity. The Anuak are already postmodern liberals in Rorty's definition, we will see, because they listen to arguments, express their views, refuse to go where false views lead them, and then when it grows clear that someone might be hurt because of his or her false views, they hurl themselves into what they believe to be the wrong choice to preserve their own sense of solidarity. Evans-Pritchard mistakenly views the Anuak as not possessing the quality of leadership, but they follow him not because they are weak or because he is such a good leader but because they want to stay together, and they will stay together even at the cost of going where they do not want to go.

We find a strong residue in Evans-Pritchard of the attitude that Geertz calls viewing others as alternatives to us. Evans-Pritchard sees the Anuak as more different from himself than they see him from themselves. This is why he is willing to endanger them by dragging them into a battle that they do not want to fight, and why they are so willing to fight for him when they do not want to fight.

Here Comes Everyman

Today I sometimes wonder if I was not attracted to anthropology, however unwittingly, by a structural affinity between the civilisations which are its subject matter and my own thought processes. My intelligence is neolithic. (Lévi-Strauss, cited by Geertz 1973, 345)

The best evidence against relativism is . . . the very activity of anthropologists, while the best evidence for relativism [is] in the writings of anthropologists. . . . In retracing their steps [in their works], anthropologists transform into unfathomable gaps the shallow and irregular cultural boundaries they had not found so difficult to cross [in the field], thereby protecting their own sense of identity, and providing their philosophical and lay audience with just what they want to hear. (Sperber, cited by Geertz 1984, 274)

The next phase in the anthropological understanding of otherness is captured in part by Lévi-Strauss and Dan Sperber, although, historically, they do not represent the attitude in its dominant phase. Lévi-Strauss's structuralism promises to reveal the universal nature of the mind and, on this basis, to make the argument for the truth of cosmopolitanism. It is not that Lévi-Strauss has a Neolithic intellect; it is, rather, that we all possess the same type of intellect. His invocation of the Neolithic intellect is a rhetorical flourish meant to dissipate any sense that so-called primitive people are more primitive, inferior than, or inherently different from Westerners. Sperber, for his part, is simply upset at ethnographers who have had an experience of universalism among natives and deny it for the love of oddity.

Geertz opposes this view because it allows no possibility of "alternative," no "use" for diversity, since diversity does not really exist. Rorty opposes this view because it attempts to found solidarity on a universal and objective truth about the mind rather than on the desire for solidarity in itself.

Ethnographers in the Missionary Position

The trouble begins with uneasy reflections on the involvement of anthropological research with colonial regimes during the heyday of Western imperialism and with its aftershadows now; reflections themselves brought on by accusations, from Third World intellectuals about the field's complicity in the division of humanity into those who know and decide and those who are known and are decided for, that are especially disturbing to scholars who have so long regarded themselves as the native's friend, and still think they understand him better than anyone else, including perhaps himself. (Geertz 1985a, 624)

Here Geertz traces the historical reason for our abandonment of cosmopolitanism. Once upon a time we saw that our attempt to find signs of human progress or of universality in human nature coincided with colonial expansion, and we wondered whether the first was not merely a rationalization for the second. The historical engine for this change begins in the anthropological spirit of Western culture, which opens its ears to the other to hear the universal. Once our ears were open, we could not fail to hear other people complaining that we were oppressing them.

The Deconstruction of the Other Is the Price of Truth

Objectivity is constituted by excluding the views of those who do not count as sane and rational men: women, children, poets, prophets, madmen. (Culler, cited by Rorty 1991, 2:119–20)

I offer Jonathan Culler's words as an example of the anthropological worry that we oppress others in our quest for truth taken to the extreme where we question not only our objectivity but the status of objectivity itself. Because we see that our truths are constructed by excluding others, we suppose that all truth is constructed by exclusion. The net result is the alienation of objectivity from solidarity on the current philosophical scene.

Hint: the great task of ethics as a science is therefore to find the truth of solidarity without alienating the concept of solidarity. Or, to rephrase, can we conceive of a community that would not be guilty of excluding in the name of its own truth? The great task of politics is to survive in the face of ethical theory by having its cake and eating it too, by finding a practical way of preserving community while reducing the violence of community.

If You Can't Beat 'Em Join 'Em

The gap between a familiar "we" and an exotic "they" is a major obstacle that can only be overcome through some form of participation in the world of the Other. . . . To my eyes funeral laments, black mourning dress, and exhumation rites *were* exotic. Yet . . . I was conscious at all times that it is not just Others who die. . . . When the brother of the deceased entered the room, the women . . . began to sing a lament about two brothers who were violently separated. . . . I thought of my own brother and cried. The distance between Self and Other had grown small indeed. (Danforth, cited by Geertz 1985b, 14–15)

Finding in the other an alternative to us can be a form of loathing the other. In Malinowski's diaries, for example, we discover an ugly disgust with natives: "On the whole my feelings toward the natives are decidedly tending to 'Exterminate the brutes'" (cited by Geertz 1985b, 74). But Malinowski also possessed an enormous, ethical self-loathing, which allowed him to invent the I-witness phase of anthropology. Here, by plumbing the depths of his or her soul, the ethnographer overcomes repulsion to natives and accepts their point of view. Malinowski, however, often turned the desire to beat natives to self-flagellation in the process.

The Subject and Other Subjects

The result is the encounter between a Self and an Other *pace* Danforth. The desire to capture the otherness of the Other isolates alterity in the realm of the capital letter. The requirement that the self represent a super Other creates the need for a super Self. The desire to represent one's own sincerity and self-loathing writes the Self with a capital letter. At this point the autobiography of the ethnographer seems to grow more important than the experience of the native.

Diary Disease

The question of signature, the establishment of an authorial presence within a text, has haunted ethnography from very early on, though for the most part it has done so in a disguised form. Disguised, because it has been generally cast not as a narratological issue, a matter of how best to get an honest story honestly told, but as an epistemological one, a matter of how to prevent subjective views from coloring objective facts. (Geertz 1985b, 9)

Although Geertz wishes to see the problem of autobiography as inherent to ethnographic writing, he understands that it has become more aggravated in recent years. The problem begins because the ethnographer must convince readers of his or her moral purpose in order to avoid accusations of ethnocentrism. (Lévi-Strauss rightly understands the father of anthropology to be Rousseau in *The Confessions.*) But once the subject grows in importance, the object begins to disappear. Ethnographers no longer court sincerity through confession. They rediscover a way to comprehend themselves by detour of the other. The field trip becomes a crucible of adversity in which suffering forges a new self for ethnographers. As soon as this happens, they may be accused of using the other as a means to an end, and ethnography as a whole falls into disrepute. Nevertheless, this development does not put an end to self-loathing and self-aggrandizement. It becomes mandatory to curse anthropology at the opening of a piece of ethnographic writing: anthropology, writes Dwyer, is "dishonest . . . pernicious and self-serving" (cited by Geertz 1985b, 95). In short, anthropology turns into a skeptical science designed to expose the worst features of the West—which is best exemplified by anthropology itself—and ethnographers become martyrs to this paradoxical and skeptical program. They go native—oppressing natives—in order to win the authority to denounce themselves as examples of Western ethnocentrism. If they do not go native, they are more guilty of ethnocentrism. The fate of anthropologists is to victimize others or themselves, but both spectacles of violence are staged for the edification of Western culture.

Finding Somewhere to Stand

> The signature issue, as the ethnographer confronts it, or as it confronts the ethnographer, demands both the Olympianism of the unauthorial physicist and the sovereign consciousness of the hyperauthorial novelist, while not in fact permitting either. The first brings charges of words but not the music, and, of course, of ethnocentrism. The second brings charges of impressionism, of treating people as puppets, of hearing music that doesn't exist, and, of course, of ethnocentrism. (Geertz 1985b, 10)

The fact that every option for the ethnographer leads to ethnocentrism reveals that ethnocentrism has become synonymous with ethnography. The result, as Geertz phrases it, is that "the very right to write—to write ethnography—seems at risk" (1985b, 133). Part of the problem is that the ethnographer cannot find a place to stand where he or she will not be made to experience the moral dilemma of writing about members of the community as if they do not belong to the community. "The gap," Geertz explains, "between engaging others where they are and representing them where they aren't, always immense, but not much noticed, has suddenly become extremely visible" (Geertz 1985b, 130). In brief, we are no longer able to talk behind someone's back because there is no place to get behind. The world is small, and the cosmopolitan imperative to think of the world as nonexclusive, as a supercommunity, is powerful.

Hint: here we may begin to see a connection to the debate about multiculturalism. Anthropology gets to the point where the differences between cultures begin to disappear. The world grows so small that it makes no sense to view the world as an ensemble of discrete cultural enclaves bordering on one another. The cosmopolitan point of view wins out and paves the way for current descriptions of individual nations, in which each in itself becomes a reflection of what used to be world culture. The world is made up of many different cultures, each of which is a miniature, multicultural version of the world.

The Quiddities of Objects; or, The French Will Never Eat Salted Butter

It is necessary to note another option used to avoid the accusation of ethnocentrism. We may resuscitate the idea of objectivity in two forms, scientific or social. In the scientific version, anthropology turns into physical anthropology and pins its desire to be nonethnocentric on the objective character of its objects. In short, social anthropology is abandoned. In the social version of objectivity, ethnographers try to isolate the objective qualities of different cultural practices, cataloguing them in order to define the integrity of the object. Reciprocity between researcher and object is strictly prohibited.

Waddling In; or, In Our Confusion Is Our Strength

Given the false choice between rigor and malaise, Geertz (1985a) proposes that anthropologists recognize that theirs is a discipline in which the quest for an object of knowledge introduces moral dilemmas about knowledge, and that this state is the real object of knowledge for anthropology. Ethnographers can no longer claim to be masters of all that they survey. Nor can they salvage the discipline by promoting hand-wringing. That there is no place to stand in anthropology exposes the fact that the ground is rather soft to begin with. Better, then, to accept that ethnographers have to waddle in, and that their confusion in the field is the best knowledge to be had.

Muddling Through

Although Rorty is critical of Geertz's fondness for "waddling in," he makes a strong case for a similar position. In "Solidarity or Objectivity?" he defends the concept of rationality as "criterionless muddling through" (1991, 1:28). We will eventually see that true rationality for him means nonviolence. My immediate goal, however, is to understand better how ethnocentrism fits with muddling through and the rejection of objectivity. Rorty recognizes that the desire for community is fundamental to human beings, but he believes that we have come to a point where we may abandon some methods of achieving it. One method is objectivity, which, for Rorty, does not actually involve foundations or empirical truths but a tactic for achieving as much intersubjective agreement as possible. Consequently, objectivity refers only to the grounds of agreement that a community recognizes as its basis. Truth is, in Rorty's definition, "what is good for *us* to believe," with the accent on "us" (1:22). In other words, truth is a "collective representation" in Durkheim's sense of the term. The truth of the clan is the clan itself.

It would appear that Rorty's definition of truth is completely political. Meaning is rooted in an existing community or group, and the ability to share beliefs defines community. Ethics possesses no universal basis; it is ethnocentric and political: "To be ethnocentric is to divide the human race into the people to whom one must justify one's beliefs and the others. The first group—one's *ethnos*—comprises those who share enough of one's beliefs to make fruitful conversation possible. In this sense, everybody is ethnocentric when engaged in actual debate, no matter how much realist rhetoric about objectivity he produces" (1991, 1:30). If we refuse to talk to Nazis, it is because we do not believe that we share enough premises to make the conversation fruitful. Conversations and narratives form the words of a tribe, and whether we belong to that tribe or wish to belong will determine how intelligible the conversations and narratives are.

I do want to mark an exception to Rorty's ethnocentric definition of ethics. Occasionally, he appears to separate the desire for community as such from the desire to belong to a specific community. The latter desire makes moral choice wholly political and ethnocentric because a person must accept the beliefs of a particular community. The former desire, however, takes on an almost cosmopolitan cast of mind. Consider, for example, the attitude of the pragmatist philosopher, no doubt Rorty himself: "As a partisan of solidarity, his account of the value of cooperative human inquiry has only an ethical base, not an epistemological or metaphysical one" (1991, 1:24). If I read this tricky statement correctly, Rorty appears to have discovered a criterion in a criterionless world: it is solidarity itself. Consequently, it grows difficult to separate his views from those of the cosmopolitan thinkers whom he usually criticizes. For once he embarks on the road to solidarity for its own sake, it is hard to stop short of cosmopolitanism. Cosmopolitan thinkers desire to create what Rorty calls a "supercommunity" rather than to maintain their own ethnic and political group. In fact, they tend to condemn existing political bodies for falling short of their ideal utopian supercommunity. This trend may still be found today among Marxist thinkers. Rorty attacks Frank Lentricchia, for example, for concluding that we live in an unreasonable society (1989a, 199). Unreasonable compared to what, Rorty responds, indicating his sense that Lentricchia has left political reality behind in favor of a cosmopolitan ideal. But Rorty's attack against the objectivist inclinations of cosmopolitan philosophy suffers from the same problem. He claims that "the traditional Western metaphysico-epistemological way of firming up our habits simply isn't working anymore" (33).

Compared to what?

In the end, when Rorty moves to give an ethical base—expressed as the desire for solidarity in itself—to human cooperative inquiry, he embraces the utopian ideal of the supercommunity discovered by the Enlightenment. His sole difference—and herein lies his ethnocentrism—is that he locates this utopian spirit in the existing political structure of Western democracies, suggesting that a supercommunity will be formed only if other groups can be persuaded to accept this spirit and to annex themselves to these polities.

Truths Aren't True Because They Work; They Work Because They Are True

Further notes on this slogan of objectivism: objectivists are objectionable because they prefer objectivity to solidarity, which is to say that they mistake their desire for solidarity as a desire for truth. Skeptics are objectionable because in their opposition to objectivists they embrace positions that are elitist and nondemocratic. In short, they misread the desire for solidarity at the heart of the objectivist's dream as false argument and sacrifice their own desire for solidarity to attack the "false" logic by which objectivists reach consensus, thereby destroying the possibility of consensus. According to Rorty, objectivists and skeptics alike embrace a version of truth that alienates it from solidarity.

But there is something paradoxical about Rorty's attitude toward objectivity. If it is, in his mind, a strategy for achieving solidarity and if this strategy has led to the emergence of the Western democracies, why bother to refute it? It appears that objectivity is our best method for creating community. Rorty has not yet escaped his philosopher's love of the truth. He wants, in Geertz's phrase, "an honest story honestly told": the desire for solidarity rendered as a form of self-conscious philosophy.

Anything Goes That Works

Rorty's critique of Lyotard on postmodernism may clarify further the pragmatic position. In *The Postmodern Condition*, Lyotard defines postmodernism as the rejection of the grand narrative explanations found at the heart of the sciences and social sciences. Once these grand narratives began to erode, according to Lyotard, it became increasingly difficult to place morality on objective grounds, and postmodernism began to emerge as an alternative. It is no accident that Geertz also holds the unraveling of grand narratives responsible for the moral hypochondria of ethnographers in the field. When the grand narrative of natural history disappeared, ethnographers had no master plan with which to organize their small and exotic narratives about encountering otherness. They lost their justification for encountering others, as well as any standard by which to differentiate themselves from others, and yet a lingering impression of otherness haunted them.

At first, Rorty accepts Lyotard's definition of postmodernism because it looks like a version of antifoundationalism. Rorty sees in Lyotard's idea of the grand narrative the cosmopolitan desire to ground truth in objectivity rather than in solidarity. Eventually, however, it becomes clear to Rorty that Lyotard is attacking not only grand narratives but narrative itself. Lyotard, according to Rorty, is "so afraid of being caught up in one more metanarrative" that he cannot bring himself to say "we" long enough "to identify with the culture of the generation" to which he belongs (1991, 2:174). Lyotard is a skeptic because he is more interested in deconstructing objectivity than in having solidarity. The Left in general suffers from this form of skepticism, according to Rorty, and since Lyotard comes from the Left, he is a double skeptic: "Lyotard unfortunately retains one of the Left's silliest ideas—that escaping from institutions is automatically a good thing, because it insures that one will not be 'used' by the evil forces which have 'co-opted' these institutions. Leftism of this sort necessarily devalues consensus and communication, for insofar as the intellectual remains able to talk to people outside the avant-garde she 'compromises' herself" (1991, 2:175). For Lyotard, "community" is a dirty word. It expresses an ethnocentric desire that leads straight to oppression, violence, Nazism.

In the debate with Lyotard, Rorty realizes that narrative is a foundationalism that works for solidarity, although he is reluctant to admit that foundationalism may be a narrative that works for solidarity as well. In this last respect, Rorty remains a skeptic, and he falls short of his own best slogan: "Anything goes that works."

Going, Going, Gone Postmodern

There is no synoptic view of culture which is more than a narrative account of how various cultures managed to get to where they now are. All of us who want big broad pictures are contributing to such an account. If we could see ourselves *as* doing that, then we would worry less about having general principles which justify our procedures. Pragmatism declines to provide us with such principles. But it does tell a story about why we thought we needed such principles, and it offers some suggestions about what a culture might be like in which we did *not* think this. (Rorty 1991, 1:92)

The Subject and Other Subjects

What This Culture Looks Like; or, Postmodern America

Both Jefferson and Dewey described America as an "experiment." If the experiment fails, our descendants may learn something important. But they will not learn a philosophical truth, any more than they will learn a religious one. They will simply get some hints about what to watch out for when setting up their next experiment. Even if nothing else survives from the age of the democratic revolutions, perhaps our descendants will remember that social institutions *can* be viewed as experiments in cooperation rather than as attempts to embody a universal and ahistorical order. It is hard to believe that this memory would not be worth having. (Rorty 1991, 1:196)

Multiculturalism

Misunderstanding America

There is no common American culture as is claimed by the defenders of the status quo. There is a hegemonic culture to be sure, pushed as if it were a common culture. (Asante 1992, 308)

Sine Qua Nons

In 1988, the unigeneric and monocultural vision of the world is insufficient. Syncretism, interdisciplinarianism, and multi-ethnicity are sine qua nons of contemporary art. And the artist or intellectual who doesn't comprehend this will be banished and his or her work will not form part of the great cultural debates of the continent. (Gómez-Peña 1988, 131)

No Thank You, Massa!

What gives is that the voice of the dominant culture has never understood what it *actually* means when it so graciously legislates racial, sexual and gender equality. Subconsciously, they think they're giving everyone a chance to be like them. A chance to live like white men. (Durand 1989, 41)

The Future of Anti-Ethnocentrism

What we are talking about here is no less than transforming the University into a center of multicultural learning: anything less continues a system of education that ultimately reproduces racism and racists. (Gordon and Lubiano 1992, 257)

Ethnocentrism is a *caché* word for the problem of racism within anthropology. The debate about multiculturalism is fundamentally about race and racism. This fact continues to be hidden but less successfully than in the anthropological context. *Multiculturalism* as a term continues to reflect the tradition of our anthropological culture in which differences are represented in terms of distinct kinds or enclaves, each possessing the type of value and coherence assigned to notions of culture, the cultural, and the cultivated. But it shifts these descriptions of value and coherence to the political context of the United States, and it is in a political context that multiculturalism will succeed or fail. It asks who is to be let into the American community and on what basis. It exposes the fact that the United States is the site of a conflict over its own self-image. Which ethnocentrism is acceptable as the ideal of this particular community? Do we want a "particular community"? What is to be the ethnic composition of this community? Which is more important, ethnic composition as such or community as such?

How Could You Do Such a Thing?

A black woman of some eminence who had recently come to the university ... announced in advance that her question was to be hostile, "a very hostile one in fact." She then said something like the following: For the first thirteen pages of your paper you talked only about white European males. Thereafter, on page 14, you mention some names of non-Europeans. "How could you do such a thing?" (Said 1992, 171)

Edward Said laments that he could elicit this response, after having worked so hard to describe the terms by which one culture might exclude and misrepresent another. His experience does tell us one thing: that an ethic of the victim has taken precedence over all others. It is difficult to make an assertion that does not victimize someone. The issue becomes who is a victim and who is not, and who is to say.

The Victim Shall Be the Hero

Whether we are speaking about the so-called victim's revolution on campus (the attempt by university officials to legislate against hate speech and to provide niches for historically disenfranchised groups) or "victim's rights" in the courtroom, it is evident that "victims" have become enormously important in our society. Multiculturalism attempts to provide a vision of the variety of people composing American society by taking a series of steps. First, it describes the disparity between a "mythic" and "hegemonic" vision of American culture and the variegated texture of the actual society. Second, it represents the victims in American society as its heroes, often claiming that they are sacrificed to the ideal of a common culture. Suffering becomes the measure of heroism. Heroic models now include not only ethnic representatives but the handicapped, the abused, the recovering addict, the scandalized politician or clergy in addition to more traditional choices such as the soldier, the athlete, the talented artist or scientist (Hughes 1992).

The idea of the victim has always provided a tacit model for ethical behavior, and now it has found its originary significance. That the victim has become a hero reveals that ethics is about including the excluded at all cost. It also reveals that the avoidance of cruelty and violence lies at the heart of ethical thought. This is a remarkable advancement in the self-consciousness of ethics. For the idea that anyone can be a victim and that all victims are heroes lays a powerful moral groundwork for the creation of a nonexclusive community of human beings. The problem, however, is in the application of the ethic of the victim. First, when any difference associated with a person may be viewed as the grounds for exclusion, it becomes difficult to legislate good and bad differences. Legislation itself becomes an offense against ethics. Second, once the ethic of the victim comes into power, it is nearly impossible to deny that someone is a victim without being accused of victimizing him or her. The worst thing that anyone can do on the present scene is to deny that someone is a victim, if he or she makes the claim.

Hint: if we accept that politics involves legislation, we will begin to see why ethics and politics are opposed on the current scene.

Lions and Christians

I should've realized she'd be dangerous when she told me how, when she was a kid, when her mother showed her a picture in a book, of lions eating Christians in a Roman stadium, she burst out crying, and when her mother asked why, she pointed to one lion and whimpered, "Look, this one hasn't got a Christian." (Kasper 1992)

Look at it from the lion's point of view. Is it fair that he doesn't have a Christian? How do we ease his suffering? How are we to right this wrong?

What does it mean to give to the victim the lion's share of ethics?

I'm OK, You're OK

I am a native of India who came to the United States in 1978. . . . A month or so after I arrived in the United States and enrolled, as a Rotary exchange student, in a public high school in Arizona, my host parents urged me to take someone from my class to the Homecoming dance. At first I was reluctant, but finally agreed. I approached a pretty young woman who said that she would have to ask her parents but would let me know tomorrow.

The next day I asked, "What did they say?"

She looked at me, "Who?"

"Your parents," I said.

"Say about what?"

At first I was simply astounded, but then I realized, with a sinking feeling, that I had approached the *wrong girl.* . . . I thought all white women looked alike. (D'Souza 1991, 22)

D'Souza's argument about education uses scare tactics. He warns that stressing victim's rights leads to a distortion of value and truth. He asks, in effect, which is more important, freedom of speech and truth or victim's rights, when he understands that most people will uphold the former values as a matter of tradition. A kind description would label him a "communitarian," a thinker who believes in the ultimate importance of community but argues that political communities are no better than their philosophical ideals (cf. Rorty 1991, 1:178). He supports the idea of a multicultural society as long as it "emphasizes what Matthew Arnold called the best that has been thought and said" (D'Souza 1992, 31). In short, he wants to win solidarity through objectivity. An unkind description, however, would locate D'Souza's agenda in the context of the civil-rights movement.

Why does D'Souza open his critique of American education with this fable about trying to date a white woman? Is D'Souza a black man who is white enough to tell us that those black people who do not want to be white are too black to be white? Listen, I know that you can't tell us apart. Well, I'm here to tell you that we can't tell you apart either.

Is it an accident that D'Souza reminds his audience that he is black and then proceeds to attack affirmative action and Afrocentrism? He represents himself as a "reasonable" person who embraces the American dream of the melting pot: "Non-Western cultures have produced great works that are worthy of study, and I think young people should know something about the rise of Islamic fundamentalism" (D'Souza 1992, 31). Judge us by the content of our character, not by the color of our skin, he seems to say; affirmative action and civil rights are wrong to judge by the color of our skin. We are supposed to understand that affirmative action and civil rights have betrayed their own best principles.

Multiculturalism in D'Souza's usage and elsewhere is a metaphor used to repress the idea of civil rights. (Only the idea of civil rights remains; as a political movement, it has ceased to exist.) For multiculturalism plays out the terms of civil rights in a different arena, now twice removed from politics, where those who have had their civil rights taken away can be kept out of the argument. One has to deny a great deal of suffering and cruelty in the world in order to frame injustice in terms of literary canons, authors' reputations, and university politics. One has to get to the university before debating whether multiculturalism prepares Americans for a wider world or narrows academic freedom, and this fact effectively excludes those for whom the debate is most important: the racially excluded, the underprivileged, and the poor of this country. That D'Souza brings up the topic of civil rights at all is a mystery. For he could conduct his entire argument solely in terms of how the demands of black students threaten the education of white, middle-class students. A case of the return of the repressed?

You're Not What You Thought You Were

> In order for me to live, I decided very early that some mistake had been made somewhere. I was not a "nigger" even though you called me one. But if I was a "nigger" in your eyes, there was something about *you*—there was something *you* needed. . . . So where we are now is that a whole country of people believe I'm a "nigger," and I *don't*, and the battle's on! Because if I am not what I've been told I am, then it means that *you're* not what you thought *you* were *either!* And that is the crisis. (Baldwin 1988, 8)

James Baldwin's words situate the debate about multiculturalism in its true context. It is not about philosophical ideals, objectivity, or education. It is about the racial composition of the United States and the myths supporting the idea of race.

Afrocentrism

Why is the worst of multiculturalism always black? Why is Afrocentrism pictured as defeating true American multiculturalism in the name of separatism? D'Souza: "But when you examine in detail the specific currents of multiculturalism, you realize that they operate to the effect of distorting non-Western cultures. You must have heard about this trend called Afrocentricity" (D'Souza 1992, 33).

Step 1 for Allan Bloom: "Sexual adventurers like Margaret Mead and others who found America too narrow told us that not only must we know other cultures and learn to respect them, but we could also profit from them. We could follow their lead and loosen up, liberating ourselves from the opinion that our taboos are anything other than social constraints. . . . All teachers of such openness had either no interest in or were actively hostile to the Declaration of Independence and the Constitution" (1987, 33).

Step 2 for Allan Bloom: "Picture a thirteen-year-old boy sitting in the living room of his family home doing his math assignment while wearing his Walkman headphones or watching MTV. . . . A pubescent child whose body throbs with orgasmic rhythms; whose feelings are made articulate in hymns to the joys of onanism or the killing of parents. . . . In short, life is made into a nonstop, commercially prepackaged masturbational fantasy" (1987, 55).

Step 3 for Allan Bloom, April 1969, Cornell University: "The professors, the repositories of our best traditions and highest intellectual aspirations, were fawning over what was nothing better than rabble. . . . The provost . . . hoped there would soon be better communication with the radical black students. . . . But for the time being the administration had to wait to hear what the blacks wanted, in the expectation that tensions could be reduced. . . . The faculty of the College of Arts and Sciences received a memorandum from its dean informing the members that . . . all were indeed institutional racists; classes for blacks only were established; the house that was being held by right of conquest was accorded to its new inhabitants by consent; a lavishly funded black studies center was established in the faculty appointments to which the black students were to have a voice" (1987, 313–316n11).

Neither D'Souza's complaint that Afrocentrism distorts non-Western cultures nor Bloom's implied history of the fall of the American university is conceivable outside an anthropological context. The first uses the spirit of anti-ethnocentrism to attack multiculturalism. The second accuses anthropology of poisoning Western culture by bringing in foreign bodies from without. Both blame blacks for the decline of the ideals of Western culture.

Traveling Agents; or, When in Rome Do as the Romans

> Imagine a young person walking through the Louvre or the Uffizi, and you can immediately grasp the condition of his soul. In his innocence of the stories of Biblical and Greek or Roman antiquity, Raphael, Leonardo, Michelangelo, Rembrandt and all the others can say nothing to him. All he sees are colors and forms—modern art. In short, like almost everything else in his spiritual life, the paintings and statues are abstract. No matter what much of modern wisdom asserts, these artists counted on immediate recognition of their subjects and, what is more, on their having a powerful meaning for their viewers. . . . Without those meanings, and without their being something essential to the viewer as a moral, political and religious being, these works lose their essence. . . . One of the most flattering things that ever happened to me as a teacher occurred when I received a postcard from a very good student on his first visit to Italy, who wrote, "You are not a professor of political philosophy but a travel agent." (Bloom 1987, 63)

Only in an anthropological context may we understand Bloom's rendering of travel as soul-adventuring among the masterpieces of Western culture. Only in the West could visiting a museum be seen as a substitute for travel. For it is Western culture that originally conceives of traveling to other worlds to satisfy an aesthetic desire for self-enrichment. The museum is the natural consequence of this desire. It provides the self with material for its aesthetic education.

Hint: that Bloom is interested in "soul" is not an ironic comment, I take it, on the ethnic meaning of the word. Nevertheless, the traditional and ethnic meanings of the word reveal a similar aesthetic sensibility with regard to the self. It is no accident that an idea of "soul" was created to refurbish the ethnic identity of African Americans. It provided an aesthetic necessary to their self-transformation and self-respect.

Naughty Words; or, E Pluribus Unum

> "Transcendent," like "universalist," is a naughty word for the politically correct multiculturalist largely because, if taken seriously, it suggests that the qualities that unite us as human beings are more important than the contingencies that separate us as social and political agents. (Kimball 1992, 69)

Roger Kimball rightly understands, I believe, the multiculturalist's quarrel with cosmopolitan vocabulary to be founded on the issue of whether unity or difference has first importance. He seems, however, not to understand that the multiculturalist's preference for difference serves a cosmopolitan morality not unlike his own. When I read a work by a black woman author, says one multiculturalist, "I do not enter into a transcendent human interaction but instead become more aware of my whiteness and maleness, social categories that shape my being" (Kimball 1992, 69). The preference for difference creates greater self-consciousness, another self-image, which is represented as a new self created by the multicultural spirit and then put in the service of a social and political critique. This new self recognizes peoples and groups who have been victimized and works for a nonexclusive community of human beings. Multiculturalism appears to work toward an experience of solidarity in the political world rather than possessing it in the aesthetic world, but, in some sense, its idea of solidarity remains "aesthetic" because it always produces an aesthetic object. Either it makes difference into an object called the multicultural self or it frames diversity as a spectacle or object to be appreciated in itself.

This is not a criticism.

Pretending to Be Natives or Colonial Administrators?

In its duplicitous, masquerading way, reading will permit us to enter other worlds. However, a multicultural reading will keep us on guard against pretending to be natives, colonial administrators, or tourists on sun-swept isles. (Stimpson 1992, 46)

As Catherine Stimpson's words suggest, multicultural reading is endowed with a redemptive force. It is all things to all people: the saving grace. It will permit the experience of otherness without, however, tempting us to pretend that we are other than we are. Finally, it will reveal our true self.

It is not clear whether multicultural reading politicizes the aesthetic experience or aestheticizes the political experience. Whatever the case, its product, the multicultural self, possesses the oracular dimension frequently created when politics and aesthetics are combined.

If literary critics and readers take the next step and begin to recount how they discovered their true self in multicultural reading and what that true self is, we will have rediscovered the "diary disease" of the anthropologist and the soul-adventuring among masterpieces of Bloom. Here the latent aestheticism of multicultural reading reveals its similarity to traditional varieties of aestheticism.

When the Left and Right begin to collapse into the same position, it is a sign that something is either very bad or very good.

Some Conclusions about This Badness and Goodness

What Books Would You Take to a Desert Island?

In America today, the underlying assumption behind the canon debate is that the books on the list are the only books that are going to be read and if the list is dropped, *no* books are going to be read. Becoming a textbook is a book's only chance—all sides take that for granted. And so all sides agree not to mention certain things that they themselves, as highly educated people and, one assumes, devoted readers, know perfectly well. For example, that if you read only twenty-five, or fifty, or a hundred books, you can't understand them, however well-chosen they are. (Pollitt 1992, 207)

Katha Pollitt's point is central. The debate over multiculturalism is not about education because both sides understand that education in the United States is not substantial enough to have any real effect on the self-image of American society. The debate over multiculturalism is really about civil rights and the political trials brought about by our failure to create an integrated society. This society cannot be created—if indeed anyone really wants to create it—by the educational establishment alone. It requires massive effort on many other fronts by the federal and state governments. It requires a Marshall Plan for the United States. The shifting of the debate about racial difference to ethnic difference and about civil rights to multicultural education is one of the great failings of the last three decades. It is a subterfuge designed to conceal the awesome irresponsibility of our political leadership. In the worst light, it blames the educational establishment for the failures of the political establishment and makes a scapegoat of the university. In the best light, it tries to solve the nation's racial problems on the cheap by working from the top down rather than from the bottom up.

Anthropology, My Fröhliche Wissenschaft

Anthropology is the best support from which to launch the ethical program of the future because it accepts the Enlightenment's definition of the anthropological as a rational comprehension of the human but realizes it as a practical encounter with the diverse peoples of the human race. It also has the advantage of having worried more about the encounter between different ethnic factions than any other discipline. Anthropology is the discipline most concerned about whether encounters with others victimize them. It is the guardian of the future because its spirit is fundamentally ethical rather than political. No matter how hard anthropologists try—no matter how great their self-loathing, caution about the quiddities of their objects, and denial of cosmopolitan morality—they cannot escape a fundamental optimism and hopefulness about the future of difference. Their reason for being is to understand difference, and their hope is that their activities will result in a better world. Whenever we need an ethics, we can turn to anthropology.

Be Yourself; or, When in Rome Do as You Done in Milledgeville

> We cannot leap outside our Western social democratic skins when we encounter another culture, and we should not try. All we should do is to get inside the inhabitants of that culture long enough to get some idea of how we look to them, and whether they have any ideas we can use. That is also all they can be expected to do on encountering us. If members of the other culture protest that this expectation of tolerant reciprocity is a provincially Western one, we can only shrug our shoulders and reply that we have to work by our own lights, even as they do, for there is no supercultural observation platform to which we might repair. The only common ground on which we can get together is that defined by the overlap between their communal beliefs and desires and our own. (Rorty 1991, 1:212–13)

Rorty provides the politics on which the future of difference rests. He is not interested in ethics (apparently), although he is interested in the future, which may be enough. He recommends that we should not ask questions that we have to climb out our own minds to answer (1991, 1:7). I call Rorty's view political because it places the *polis* first and attends to intracultural differences before all others. Rorty's *polis* is a Western democracy, the United States, and he would rather abandon the ethic of anti-ethnocentrism than the politics of democracy because he believes that the specific ethnocentrism of American democracy is at heart anti-ethnocentric.

The Ethnocentric Horn of the Dilemma

The pragmatists' justification of toleration, free inquiry, and the quest for undistorted communication can only take the form of a comparison between societies which exemplify these habits and those which do not, leading up to the suggestion that nobody who has experienced both would prefer the latter. It is exemplified by Winston Churchill's defense of democracy as the worst form of government imaginable, except for all the others which have been tried so far. (Rorty 1991, 1:29)

Rorty recommends that we grasp the ethnocentric horn of the dilemma rather than the relativist or skeptical one because the latter two condemn any hope for the future of particular political communities.

No matter how much pragmatists try—no matter how great their inherent isolationism, disappointment in democracy, and contempt for cosmopolitan morality—they cannot escape a fundamental optimism and hopefulness about the future of difference. Their reason for being is to preserve the unique features of social democracy, and their hope is that their activities will result in a better world. Whenever we need a politics, we can turn to pragmatism.

Persuasion Rather Than Force

Cosmopolitan morality is interested in resolving intercultural differences to prepare for the emergence of a supercommunity in the future. Pragmatists are interested in resolving intracultural differences to maintain the ideals of the Western democracies, in which they place their best hopes for the future of global politics. Whether we prepare for the future by embracing ethical ideas or by trying to keep political structures in place is finally less important than our attitude about how change will occur. Cosmopolitan moralists and pragmatists may emphasize different means of approaching the future, but they share two important principles. Both embrace utopian philosophies, and they believe in nonviolence. As Rorty explains it, comparing his point of view to that of the skeptical Lyotard: "for us 'rational' merely means 'persuasive,' 'irrational' can only mean 'invoking force.' . . . Even those who, like myself, think of France as the source of the most original philosophical thought currently being produced, cannot figure out why French thinkers are so willing to say things like 'May 1968 refutes the doctrine of parliamentary liberalism.' From our standpoint, nothing could refute that doctrine except some better idea about how to organize society. No event—not even Auschwitz—can show that we should cease to work for a given utopia. Only another, more persuasive, utopia can do that" (1991, 1:220).

The Good Old Days of Widow Burning and Cannibalism Are Gone Forever

Marginality and homelessness are not to be gloried in; they are to be brought to an end, so that more, and not fewer, people can enjoy the benefits of what has for centuries been denied the victims of race, class, or gender. (Said 1992, 189)

The World Is Here

"When I heard a schoolteacher warn the other night about the invasion of the American educational system by foreign curriculums," Ishmael Reed writes, "I wanted to yell at the television set, 'Lady, they're already here.' One of our most visionary politicians said that he envisioned a time when the United States could become the brain of the world, by which he meant the repository of all the latest advanced information systems. . . . Is that the kind of world we desire? . . . Or does North America deserve a more exciting destiny? To become a place where the cultures of the world crisscross. This is possible because the United States is unique in the world: The world is here" (Reed 1988, 159–60).

Counterargument 1; or, America the Beautiful

Wild applause; fireworks; music—*America the Beautiful*; all together, now: *Calvin Coolidge, Gunga Din, Peter Pan, spontaneous combustion.* Hurrah for America and the national culture! Hurrah! (Smith, cited by Searle 1992, 96)

This is Barbara Herrnstein Smith's reaction to E. D. Hirsch's program for early childhood minority education. Would she conclude as well that Ishmael Reed is a dupe of the *America the Beautiful* syndrome? Here we discover once more the limitation placed on political change by the moral hypochondria of skepticism. Skepticism is an ethics terrified of naming itself as such. It is an utter failure as a politics.

With friends like this, the civil-rights movement does not need enemies.

Counterargument 2; or, We Are Not the World

Ethnocentrism is the tyranny of Western aesthetics. An Indian mask in an American museum is transported into an alien aesthetic system where what is missing is the presence

The Subject and Other Subjects

of power invoked through performance ritual. It has become a conquered thing, a dead 'thing' separated from nature and, therefore, its power. (Anzaldúa 1988, 32)

From Anzaldúa's point of view, few encounters between the West and non-West can come to any good. There is, nevertheless, something of a one way street in her description. First, she implies that the West has no rituals that might be disenchanted in its confrontation with the non-West. The "diary disease" of anthropologists suggests otherwise. Second, she places the non-West on the side of nature and the West on the side of culture. Evans-Pritchard would no doubt agree. Third, she suggests that the Indian mask in an American museum is more alienated than, for example, a Western artifact in an native village. No doubt, the Indian coming upon a native mask in a museum will experience an emotion of vertigo and displacement similar to that of the Western anthropologist coming upon a native wearing army fatigues or carrying a Roy Rogers lunch bucket.

Counterargument 3; or, Symbolic Wounds

Paul Rabinow calls symbolic violence any disruption in native life caused by the presence of the ethnographer: "To those who claim that some form of symbolic violence was not part of their own field experience, I reply simply that I do not believe them. It is inherent in the structure of the situation" (cited by Geertz 1985b, 98).

Only the anthropological spirit of Western ethics can account for Rabinow's privileging of symbolic violence between natives and ethnographers—or intercultural difference—over a symbolic violence internal to intersubjective situations in general, whether Western or non-Western—or intracultural difference. Unless one makes a specific case for the lesser evil of intracultural violence—and such a case is not, I believe, plausible without abandoning politics—one cannot limit the concern with symbolic violence to the ethnographic encounter. Some multiculturalists, for example, have applied this same interpretation to encounters within single nations between citizens, worrying about the destruction of pockets of ethnic identity and resisting the ideal of the monoculture.

In fact, however, the notion of symbolic violence is an overreaction to the problem of violence that ends by making both ethics and politics impossible. Taken to the extreme, this interpretation holds that no contact between different groups or different persons exists that does not produce a form of symbolic violence. The domain of self and other becomes, as in Sartrean existentialism, for instance, the premier terrain of violence. Desiring to be recognized and not being recognized is a form of symbolic violence. Indifference is a crime against the other's subjectivity. Shaking hands shakes the foundations of the self.

This position has no political viability, and it is ethically incoherent.

The task, therefore, becomes to differentiate between, and to organize, forms of violence, whether physical or symbolic: to ask which types of symbolic violence are to be named as cruel, which are to be ignored and under what conditions, subject to what exceptions, and to produce a "rational" conception of violence, no matter how difficult, how inadequate, and how prone to creating its own forms of violence. The task is to form an ethically advanced culture, where advancement is defined as attempting to eliminate not only those forms of violence that brought about the need for an ethics as such but those forms of violence produced within the field of ethical deliberation (Siebers 1988, 92).

The Words of the Tribe

The ultimate question is what kind of self-image do we want for ourselves and for our community? On the one hand, ethnocentrism, as Rorty defines it, is necessary because it refuses to be disgusted by the desire for community. It gives priority to solidarity over objectivity. It also places a limit on community by providing guidelines for tolerance and exclusion: "Accommodation and tolerance," Rorty explains, "must stop short of a willingness to work within any vocabulary that one's interlocutor wishes to use, to take seriously any topic that he puts forward for discussion" (Rorty 1991, 190). In short, politics necessitates creating a shared vocabulary—the words of the tribe—for members of a polity recommend themselves to others with similar tastes and identities. Political communities cannot survive by favoring the ideals of nonmembers over those of its members. On the other hand, anti-ethnocentrism, as defined within the cosmopolitan tradition, is necessary because it provides the ideal by which we determine our choice of polity; in short, it helps to designate the ethnocentrism to which we are going to grant our loyalty. It encourages a spirit of detachment, a kind of ethnographer's *dépaysement*, with respect to our specific communities, allowing the possibility of choosing between political forms and changing existing ones. Whether we call it Kantian disinterest or a Rawlsian veil of ignorance, the ability to speak from an objective view, to express a view from nowhere in particular, protects us against the temptation to settle for what we have now instead of thinking about the future.

Cosmopolitan morality lingers, therefore, in every conceivable choice, even in the strictest pragmatist position, because its principal task is to promote the act of choice. It provides the little freedom necessary to imagine what another life would be. It allows us to consider a different set of choices. It grants us the gift of imagination, and this imagination is necessary for whatever self-image we might make up for ourselves. We need not choose between objectivity and solidarity or between truth and falsehood once we decide to choose a free society. All we need is to choose that society and that freedom again and again. They will provide us with the ladder necessary to climb to wherever we are going as well as with a way to get back down, should we discover that we are afraid of heights.

Pogo Shtick

We have met the cosmopolitan moralist and He is Us.

Reading for Character:
Where It Was, I Must Come to Be

I Cannot Do Otherwise

The persona of the critic is an enigmatic construction, if we consider the resources that are and are not permitted to it. When is a critic too personal? When is he or she too impersonal? Modern theory, thanks largely to feminism, has discovered the personal voice of the critic. But the institution of literary criticism still renders the reading experience less personal than that of common readers, who are free to fantasize about situations, to daydream, and to identify with characters, without having to confess it to anyone—or so I fantasize. The personal experiences of critics rarely figure in their acts of reading, and when they do, they are well concealed. Rather, critics tend to build their careers by creating an abstract and neutral persona to present to their audience, and this persona becomes the ego that reads, that comments on the general connections between texts, on their authors, language, and times, and on other sources of relevant information. This tendency toward an institutionalized critical ego, however, meets some resistance from critics whose reputations have grown to the point where they may present a more personal view of themselves to their readers. In the tradition of *Rousseau juge de Jean-Jacques*, celebrity critics turn inward, measure themselves, and begin to speak of the world apropos of themselves. Roland Barthes comes easily to mind as an example. Derrida also likes to write himself into his criticism, as *La Carte postale* amply demonstrates.

And yet the distance between critical and common reader may not be as great as it first appears. Perhaps the celebrity critic does not exemplify a resistance to reading as much as an exception that confirms what happens whenever a person takes up that genre of thing called a book. I take up the book and read it, and where it was, I must come to be. Prosopopoeia, of course, names the aesthetic process through which the self becomes itself by incorporating it into self. But how does a book become a self (or a self, a book)? How does an object become a subject? How does something so alien to the self as a thing become the instrument (let us not shy away from the word) by which the self becomes itself?

These types of questions are dear to any argument that privileges aesthetics as a mode of subjectivization. Rather than recounting that history here, however, I will focus on the single trope by which a thing becomes a person and ask how it functions in a book in which a self tries to avoid objectification. J. Hillis Miller's *Versions of Pygmalion* (1990) may be seen to confront the dilemma of prosopopoeia directly as soon as one understands that it is less concerned with personification as an aesthetic device than as a mode of self-fashioning. It is far less the example of virtuoso reading that we have come to expect from deconstructive critics than a vision of one critic reading. "Suppose the book I pick up and decide to read," Hillis Miller asks, "happens to be Henry James's *What Maisie Knew*. . . . What happens when I do that?" (23). Or, "what happens when I read Kleist?" (99). On the one hand, Miller wants to offer us a more intimate and imaginative persona, tying his experiences to significant moments of reading and questioning his own methodology. At several points in the argument, for example, he tries to suggest ways in which undecidability might *not* be a general property of literary language. On the other hand, Miller is arguably the person most responsible on the current scene for the institutionalization of deconstruction. It is true that he had resisted the role of pedagogue for some time, taking the requisite care to fence the idea of deconstruction within scare quotes. But in recent years he seems to have given up this resistance, going on occasion so far as to adopt the previously detested label, *deconstructionist,* to refer to his own activity. A good example of this latter trend is his little essay for the *New York Times Magazine,* "How Deconstruction Works" (1986), which provides an example of the method, when previously most deconstructionists had denied that deconstruction could ever be exemplified, let alone reduced to a methodology.

Versions of Pygmalion continues this latter trend but tries to find a different site of resistance. The book begins by defining prosopopoeia as the privileged trope of narrative because it describes the transformation by which authors, narrators, and readers bring characters to life. "Personification is the inaugural trope of narration," Miller concludes, "and without it there is no storytelling" (1990, 220–21). Prosopopoeia names the process by which something dead comes alive, by which an "it" becomes an "I," by which a character becomes a person, and Miller is right to make the case for its importance to narrative. I want to suggest, however, that a more personal drama resides in this subject matter and that the idea of Pygmalionism may, in fact, have as much to do with developments that Miller would like confront in his own career as with a general theory of reading. At a personal level, his book seems to ask whether an "I"—the private and particular response of one person to one text—can live within a method—specifically, the institution of interpretation now called deconstructionism. Another facet of prosopopoeia would appear to involve whether the reader can represent his or her own personality through the medium of a critical methodology.

Of course, that Miller chooses the myth of Pygmalion to breathe life into his critical persona in 1990 is a revealing comment on the state of deconstruction in the United States. Some have argued that the discovery of Paul de Man's Nazi connections killed deconstruction in this country, and mourning for it abounds. Miller has suffered from this turn of events perhaps more than anyone. Now his task would be to take what many consider to be a dead movement and to restore it to life, to give it a face and personality once more, to transform an "it" into an "I." His previous writings show that these are precisely the terms in which he must work. In *The Ethics of Reading,* Miller had summoned Martin Luther's words, "*Ich kann nicht anders* (I cannot do otherwise)," to describe the linguistic imperative confronting the reader of any text; the strategy of the phrase was to describe how meaning takes hold of readers in an irresistible way that has nothing to do with personal history or beliefs (1987, 4). The ego of the ethics of reading was by definition disinterested and impersonal—a Kantian neuter, an "it." It could not, Miller cautioned, make a literary text mean anything that it wanted. It was an ego that subjected itself to a general law, and the law was deconstruction. In the sequel on Pygmalionism, Miller raises the stakes. The question becomes whether he can insert himself into Luther's phrase and make it personal at the same time, whether he can write "I cannot do otherwise" without betraying a loss of vitality or making an embarrassing admission about either his own particular resourcefulness or that of deconstruction in general.

Miller's argument about prosopopoeia is therefore divided between the concerns of the living and the dead. A series of extremes—personal versus impersonal, particular versus general, theme versus structure—animates each chapter as well as the general theory of what is now called the "ethics of narrative." At one extreme, Miller demonstrates that he cares about the individual works. He promises to read each work on its own terms and to discover what seems "strange" or "unaccountable" about it. At the other extreme, Miller must discover that each text is, finally, only a version of a single meaning, most obviously because all are "versions of Pygmalion." In both cases, the imperative, *Tolle, lege,* constitutes the first law of reading. Miller submits himself to it and confesses the anguish caused to him when he must choose to read one book among many: "In order to fulfill the obligations involved in the ethics of reading, I must first read something, some one book, poem, novel, or essay, in spite of the fact that to single out one over all others is not only an arbitrary and unjustified choice, but also a betrayal of my obligation to all the other books" (20). From this moral unease about choice springs an urgency to understand what the act of reading means in the first person: "What happens when I read, when I *really* read, which does not happen all that often?" (20).

The act of reading visits Miller as surely as it does Saint Augustine, and it maintains a special meaning for him. It is a unique critical activity separate from the experience of common readers. When we read these passages, however, we should understand that we have met with the special anxieties of the modern literary critic. These anxieties are both sublime and silly. They are sublime because they are inseparable from the project of modern ethics in its most insistent form, which broods about the implications of human difference and its relation to the possibility of creating and maintaining an inclusive moral community (Siebers 1988). If it seems that Miller is thinking about books in the way that most of us should like to think about people, it is important to understand that this strange form of sympathy has a meaning, even if it seems out of place. A powerful ethical imperative to respect diversity and to avoid exclusion animates Miller's thought. It evokes through the symbolism of books the large political and moral dramas present in modern life and played out most obviously in the spheres of race and gender relations, where it means something to chose to interact with one person over another and where justifications for our choices are fraught with unease. Wayne Booth has proposed the same analogy. *The Company We Keep* takes, in effect, a maxim having to do with the human associations that we keep and self-consciously extends it to books. It founds an "ethics of fiction" on the basis of whether and how we go about rejecting books that offer us their friendship (1988, 222–23). Nevertheless, the amity of books, if it is to have any moral resonance, has to be a symbol for human community.

The ethics of reading, then, defines a rather peculiar territory, and unless we keep in mind the symbolism linking book to person, Miller's excessive guilt about choosing a book to the exclusion of others or his urgent preoccupation with whether he is really reading seems silly, if not pathological. I will suggest below that there may be every reason to call it nonsense, even though we may wish to accept the symbolism as an important representation of the terms of ethical life. A further elaboration of this symbolism involves the notion of "surprise," which is the measure for Miller by which one determines whether reading is taking place:

> Reading should be guided by the expectation of surprise, that is, the presupposition that what you actually find when you read a given work is likely to be fundamentally different from what you expected or what previous readers have led you to expect. Good reading is also guided by the presupposition of a possible heterogeneity in the text. The ever-present danger in reading is that it will not be reading at all, but just finding in the text of what the reader already knew he or she was going to find there and therefore has posed as a screen between himself or herself and the actual text. (33)

One could explain this statement with reference to modern injunctions against habitual thinking or self-fulfilling prophecies about truth and meaning. This would make reading a model of philosophical rigor, and obviously this analogy abounds everywhere on the present scene. But when one addresses "ethics" in this language, another analogy becomes irresistible: that between texts and people. Miller seems to be speaking about books as if he were referring to the prejudicial judgments that we make about other human beings. He represents reading as a way of discovering independence of mind in matters of moral judgment. At least since Kant attempted to define moral judgment on the basis of the autonomy of the reasoning subject and not on the heteronomy of the experiencing subject, the strongest command of morality has been to think for oneself (or, in Kant's language, to resist the tutelage of other people and received ideas). If we are to resist prejudice, the Enlightenment vice, we need to reflect on the radical freedom of our fellow human beings, Kant argued, and to understand that we cannot discover their true value if we see them either through other people's eyes or through our own biases (1952, §40). Kant made truth the fulcrum of morality, but we often forget that he was not referring to truth in the abstract but to truthfulness about human beings, which is why his ethics is a philosophical anthropology and not merely an orthopedic epistemology.

If we focus on the analogy between books and people or aesthetics and ethics, we may begin to understand why critical method poses such a threat to critical thinking. "The more successfully theory is institutionalized according to certain agenda," as Miller puts it, "the more successfully it may be rendered harmless" (84). The phrasing here is unfortunate, but the meaning is legible. Theory is supposed to attack impersonal, methodical, and institutionalized modes of thinking, making us aware of the ways in which they create exclusions and do violence to people. What theory purports to harm are harmful types of thought. But when theory turns methodical, it becomes as much of a force for exclusion and injustice as any other institutional mode. This is the rub that deconstruction—the theory most interested on the current scene in the harmful potential of institutional thought—faces as its own insights about the dangers of institutions grow increasingly more predictable, cliché, and institutional. At first the deconstructive *use* of a text to exemplify an exclusive mode of thinking might be justified, although only by the most utilitarian arguments. Soon, however, deconstructive reading becomes an offense against the freedom and particularity of the text. For to use anything as an example of anything else is the essential vice of representation such as deconstruction understands it. To see deconstruction as a virtue one must commit the crime that it names as the greatest vice.

This paradox explains in part why Miller wishes so desperately to represent what is unique about each work (traditionally an aesthetic goal), why he ends up making each work a version of every other (an ethical goal), and why the whole process is so ethically frustrating. It also explains his personal dilemma and why it takes the form of an opposition between the forces of "I" and "it." Deconstruction reveals that the desire for individuality and the nature of representing individuality are radically incompatible. Miller cannot avoid wishing to represent what is "strange" about a work any more than he can avoid wanting to capture what is "unique" about himself or his own act of reading. But each time that he reads, *really* reads, he discovers the blind necessity associated by deconstruction with reading. The I cannot find itself in the it, no matter how hard it looks for it. Deconstruction becomes an existential drama incapable of naming itself as such. (Indeed, are we not talking about the relation between the *en soi* and *pour soi* in Sartre's analysis?) Miller cannot go on and he cannot stop. He is caught eternally in the middle. Faced by "reading," he can only lament: "I must get on with it and begin where I can" (18). In short, he must suffer the paradox of finding an "I" where "it" was, while knowing that the discovery is itself an imposition of meaning (from nowhere) designed to bridge the unbridgeable gap between an "it" and an "I."

Under another name this paradox is simply prosopopoeia, which reveals itself always to be a "prosopopoeia of prosopopoeia" (6). That prosopopoeia is doubled against itself means that it is a figure of deconstruction as much as of fiction. Prosopopoeia is not only in Miller's usage the narrative process by which an "I" comes to be where "it" was. It is also the deconstructive trope exposing that every "I" conceals an "it." "Personification," Miller explains, "both covers over . . . blank places in the midst of life and, sooner or later, brings them into the open" (4). Deconstruction reveals that all texts are allegories of the way that their own insights about tropes cannot be read. But, as the trope of all tropes, personification is itself always already self-deconstructive: "Each prosopopoeia therefore contains in itself the traces of its inaugural violence and artifice" (222). It is only necessary that the trope fall under the gaze of those who have eyes to see it. "The law of personification," Miller explains, "is that for a *sharp reader* it uncovers as it covers over. Prosopopoeia effaces, defaces, and disfigures even as it confers, ascribes, or prescribes a face and a figure" (227; emphasis mine).

Miller creates the fiction of the "sharp reader" out of language as surely as Pygmalion carves Galatea out of marble. The problem is, of course, that prosopopoeia is necessary to the process of its own deconstruction. The figure of the sharp reader emerges as a prosopopoeia capable of understanding what prosopopoeia is. The "it," in short, becomes self-reflective without creating the alienating structure of an "I." But Miller would deny that this is possible because language mediates the existence of every "I." An "I" cannot emerge from an "it" by the force of a trope.

Personification, then, necessarily frustrates the desire to find a self within linguistic constructions, be they causal sequences, character descriptions, or critical methods. The trope names the point of infinite regress at which the subject of consciousness would represent itself as the object of consciousness and thus lose itself as subjectivity. The fiction of the "sharp reader" is a stopgap used by Miller to slow momentarily the regress in order to represent the paradox of repetition, but, of course, this personification grows deadly because we cannot read the trope without further personifying it as Miller himself. The prosopopoeia named "J. Hillis Miller" creates his critical ego by inventing the prosopopoeia of the "sharp reader" for the purpose of revealing that prosopopoeia must always fail to produce a prosopopoeia even at its most convincing moment. Since this is all too much to bear, except for the sharp reader (dull readers please have patience), most people will protect themselves against the nauseating strangeness of language by giving up the project of radical reading and seeking security in the illusion of personhood. In short, the dilemma that Miller faces is that any successful conveyance of his own critical personality must be the result of a failure of reading on the part of his audience. The most personal moments in his narrative are by definition the least believable because they emerge only by stabilizing the repetition of the reading experience.

Miller's particular interpretations merely play out this general paradox using the specific language of the work being read. In the case of James's *What Maisie Knew*, the successive personifications forming characters break down when we most need them because the narrative succumbs to meaningless repetitions. Of Maisie, Miller writes: "At the moment we most need to know what is going on in her mind, Maisie's subjectivity becomes a nonentity that no longer exists as something or someone whose story can be told according to the narrative presuppositions operative here" (1990, 72). Similarly, the narrator and James himself are nonentities because their differences are engulfed by a disgusting sameness: "The vanishing of the narrator's access to Maisie's mind . . . may lead the reader to recognize that the narrator has all along been an impersonal or neutral power of narration, 'neuter' in the sense of *ne . . . uter*, neither one nor the other, neither male nor female. In changing himself into the narrator of *What Maisie Knew* James depersonalized himself and became the narrative voice . . . (the it, the neutral)" (72). The reader of Kleist encounters another version of Pygmalionism. Kleist shows, according to Miller, that reading is a form of improvisation that defeats institutionalization; but improvisation reveals itself to be an imposition of meaning and identity necessary to institutionalization. As Miller sums it up, "the central topic of Kleist's work is the human tendency to project personal agency and concatenation on what may be a random sequence" (137). Narrative, in other words, imposes a causal sequence on, or projects a human figure into, the emptiness of ultimate loss; it is a form of resisting the mourning that is language by creating a substitute for what has died, when in fact what has been lost has never been alive in the first place. Melville's "Bartleby the Scrivener" tells the story of a character that resists personification, thereby providing an obstacle to our most precious narrative impulses. The sharp reader of the tale must recognize that Bartleby's story cannot be told because he represents a deadly sameness, an implacable neutrality; this special character disables "any attempt to put 'Bartleby the Scrivener' in its place by answering the question, 'In mercy's name, who is he?'" (174). Finally, Blanchot provides the most explicit example of Miller's theory. The oddity of Blanchot's writing derives from his desire to uncover in the process of writing itself the forcefulness of repetition, death, and nonmeaning. *L'Arrêt de mort* is a text that exposes the "itness" of narrative. It confronts the fact that narrative sentences us to death rather than to life, obsessively translating ordinary language into the foreign tongue of the "it." Blanchot's reverse Pygmalionism reveals the false variety of narrative forms. The inventiveness of narrative consists in its remarkably ability to conceal "it" behind a barrage of "I's." Consequently, for Blanchot, every story has the same meaning, although there exist infinite repetitions of this same meaning.

There is something disingenuous about Miller's initial claim, so appealing to nontheorists, that he wants to capture the individuality of texts in all their glory rather than imposing a theory upon them. He believes, it is only too clear, that the desire to express the individuality of either the critic or the text in the act of reading is a prosopopoeia, which of necessity reveals the desire for individuality to be based on a fiction. Consequently, his claim appears to be a piece of bait set to capture a wider audience for a declining method. The personal voice added to his criticism has the same effect. It pretends to humanize the inhuman nature of interpretation, such as deconstruction defines it, but this humanization is really only a prosopopoeia, which means that it merely gives the illusion of surmounting the linguistic necessity prized by deconstructive theorists but so revolting to a wider audience of practical readers. In the end, Miller saves himself from bad faith only by positing bad faith as the defining characteristic of human existence. The tragedy of human life, according to Miller, is that we must commit "a linguistic error possibly leading to social and domestic disaster" in order to come to the understanding that exposes this error (1990, 240). But this knowledge arrives too late, and the reader must take responsibility for the ethical, political, and aesthetic results of the error.

Such is Miller's definition of the ethics of reading, and he condemns ethics to exist within these limitations. Reading exposes that meaning is undecidable in the most radical sense. We cannot trace the logic by which causal sequences arise from randomness or personification changes an "it" into an "I." We cannot, consequently, justify causes and people in a satisfying or reasonable way. The ethics of reading affirms the impossibility of human agency but determines to live with our actions and judgments anyway, despite the fact that we are never responsible for them. But Miller never explains the process by which a person could assume responsibility for actions not his or her own, and the weight of his entire analysis would seem to indicate that such agency on the part of a person is only another instance of prosopopoeia, another elitist and illusory construction such as we find in the idea of the "sharp reader." Prosopopoeia demands that each writing of an "I" collapses into the "it," and in the end, Miller must fail to write himself into Martin Luther's imperative. *Ich kann nicht anders?* No. *Es kann nicht anders.*

I Must Get On with It

If modern theorists are correct, writers are always in some primary way readers of their own texts, and all narratives, whether fictional or critical, are the results of one person's private reading of an act of writing. Narratives are those places—Miller is absolutely right—where an "I" comes to be where "it" was. No doubt, this fact, if it is a fact, accounts for the many memorable comments of authors about the character whom they have become or failed to become. *Madame Bovary, c'est moi,* said Flaubert, supposedly in a moment of vertiginous triumph. But who won? Who is who? "Do you know my Tatyana has rejected Onegin?" Pushkin remarked, expressing the surprise that one generally owes to real people and not to literary characters: "I never expected it of her." Tatyana's rejection of Onegin becomes in some way a sign of Pushkin's inability to surmount Onegin. For he is as surprised by Tatyana's rejection as Onegin is. Had Pushkin understood Tatyana better, had he been able to say à la Flaubert, *Tatyana, c'est moi,* would he have died in a duel meant to salvage his honor, when only his life, not his honor, was salvageable? The potential irony in any of these identifications is beside the point because irony is the poignant confusion from which authors sometimes suffer with respect to their characters, as Nietzsche knew too well. The artist is prone to confuse himself with his character, Nietzsche argued, "as if he himself were what he is able to represent, conceive, and express. The fact is that *if* he were it, he would not represent, conceive, and express it: a Homer would not have created Achilles nor a Goethe a Faust if Homer had been an Achilles or Goethe a Faust" (1969, 101). Prosopopoeia, for Nietzsche, describes the narrative action by which a self brings itself to life in the act of bringing to life another self who knows something that it does not.

When we discuss the possibility of one self knowing something that another self does not, of one self learning from another self, or of a self learning from itself through the act of reading or writing, we recognize implicitly that prosopopoeia describes a process of identification between subjects that involves both their sameness and difference, and that the varieties of this sameness and difference are myriad and not governed by a universal law or structure. In terms of the act of reading, this means that we read not for plot but for character. Prosopopoeia is the essential narrative device because readers identify with characters, not plot, and an ethics of narrative must therefore confront the possible forms of this identification. Or, to put it another way, to be ethical, reading must concern itself with theme rather than with structure because themes organize the choices, actions, situations, and personalities of the characters—"the interest"—by which readers enter into identifications (cf. Seung 1982; Siebers 1992, 5–7, 34; Tomashevsky 1965, 62–66).

To commit oneself to an ethics of reading at the structural level, however, avoids the problem of identification. Miller makes this choice, producing a distorted notion of ethics. His is a view of character in which character does not exist. It is no accident that he does not discuss identification. Nor is it surprising that he consistently denies the importance of theme. His explicit purpose is to discover an alternative to thematics: "Is there an ethical dimension to the act of reading as such (as opposed to the expression of ethical themes in the text read)?" (1990, 13). By defining ethics at the level of reading rather than remaining within the work and its themes, Miller avoids the difficulty of defining what character is, which, I have argued elsewhere, remains the ethical problem par excellence (1992, 5–19). He also substitutes a book for a character in the process of identification. He feels guilt or shame about not choosing a book rather than feeling these passions about characters. The deconstructive method would appear to be a remedy for Miller's personal anxiety about not reading everything: it designs a mode of interpretation that makes the reading of all books unnecessary because it transforms all books into the same book.

In short, Miller defines ethics in a way that justifies the further marginalization of reading in modern society. At the very least, he defines the subject of ethics in terms of the choices that we make between books at the institutional level. Canon reform would thus emerge as the ethical domain par excellence. The ethics of reading is only about what we should or should not read. At the very most, by diminishing the ethics of reading in such a powerful way, he creates a situation in which reading can no longer be justified as an activity. If choosing to read one book excludes the reading of other books, it must certainly exclude other actions as well, actions that would appear to have far greater value than reading one single book, which, in this view, is not that different from reading any other book. If the ethics of reading consists solely, as Miller appears to define it, in the choice of reading or not, then there is no way to justify reading. Only if we admit that a reader may learn something from a book, can we justify ethically that action over another action. Knowledge cannot be located at a structural level in this argument. Nor can it take the form of the one moral appropriate to all stories, no matter how just the moral. The possibility of knowledge must exist in the themes of a book and in the ability of readers to enter into identifications with its characters. Only in this way can an ethics of reading represent the particularity and arbitrariness of moral life.

Obviously, however, there exist many obstacles to identification both in the social world and in reading literary works. There are two extremes in identification, whether we are thinking about readers or literary artists. Either the writer-reader brings the character to life (or not), making "it" into an "I," or the character brings the writer-reader to life (or not), making another "it" into an "I." We might say, using the myth of Pygmalion as a metaphor, that the writer-reader may bring the statue to life or may erect "the statue of his own ego," to paraphrase Lacan, in the place of the character (1977, 2–3). We understand that narratives fail to develop because either the writer-reader does not bring characters to life—they remain wooden—or expels characters to leave as the sole site of subjectivity his or her own ego. In the case of autobiography, to take an extreme example of the latter, the writer creates a successful narrative only by making himself or herself into a character, although the "I" of the narrative still remains something of a statue, a monument to ego.

Typically, theorists complicate the already complex process of identification by obstructing reading for character. They tend to sculpt one theory out of a narrative and erect it as a monument to the critical ego. At other times, they refer all meaning in a narrative to its author, making him or her into a statue. Each emotion of the author, in this view, aims through writing to create a statue of the emotion. Werther, for example, becomes a mock Goethe. Poe writes only about himself. Deconstructive critics obey this same law with a twist. They admit that they cannot trace the language of a narrative to an author, although they continue to refer to it using the proper name of the author (Miller, for example, repeatedly refers the "insights of language" to "Melville," "Kleist," "Blanchot," and others), but they imagine another statue in the author's place. They locate ambivalence, indecision, violence, insight, and blindness in a statue called the text. Deconstructive critics believe that morality resides in language itself, not in our relation to specific narratives. But whatever the purity of moral purpose found in textuality, such purpose is illegible and useless, I would insist, unless it is dramatized by characters in the time of a narrative. Ambivalence, indecision, violence, insight, and blindness are valuable only when they are embedded in the situations of characters with whom readers might identify.

Since most people read by identifying with characters, it does not make a great deal of sense to try to give an example of it. We already understand how it works, and an example would be too personal by the standards of institutional criticism anyway. It is only because the ethics of the common reading experience has been so severely challenged by skeptical theories of interpretation that a theory about the ethics of reading is necessary at all. Miller's theory is not this theory: he is less interested in the ethics of the reading experience than in deconstructing what has always been conceived to be the moral value in reading. The motivation for this deconstruction of ethics in the name of ethics is unclear. Certainly, it would be difficult to construct a critical personality on the basis of the everyday variety of reading. Everyday reading has no theory. It is not sharp enough. It is dull because no single moment or word has to rise out of the text that might focus all our attention, energy, and enthusiasm toward a single solution to the problems that the narrative presents to us. The text confronts us with a great diversity and many experiences. Our only choice is to read and to read again, until we can read no longer.

"Bartleby the Scrivener" is an especially powerful example of this effect. The story comes alive for me, despite the fact that most of its characters are too eccentric to identify with, because the story is about the ethical problem of living with eccentric people. The narrator is a man who understands the deepness of virtue and who fails to be virtuous in his own eyes because he cannot be as moral as he would like to be. I nevertheless judge him to be virtuous, and I wish that I could be as virtuous as he. Although Bartleby is nothing to him, he tries to shield him from persecution. He similarly indulges his other copyists, who are as odd as Bartleby. Indeed, the narrator originally hires Bartleby because he believes that the man will provide him with a welcomed respite from the ugly moods of Turkey and Nipper. The narrator has an uncommon sense of the errands of his life, and he repeatedly beats down evil impulses in himself to treat Bartleby with cruelty, although not always with success. It is true that his vanity is stroked at times by the sense of his own virtue, when he has managed to be especially tolerant of Bartleby's exasperating conduct, but it does not last for long and cannot be said to be a strong motivation. The best of intentions seems to move the narrator.

But the best of intentions is not always enough to save another person because, first, we must be able to measure up to our best intentions, second, the person whom we would like to help must be willing to accept our help, and, third, the help must be sufficient to the problem. The narrator intends to help Bartleby, but his determination slackens when he discovers that he may have to sacrifice his own life as he knows it to try to save his friend. Bartleby does not make the process easy. He refuses to act as a public person in public. He wants his preferences to the exclusion of every one else's. The narrator tolerates these preferences to the point of paying him for not working and allowing him to live at the office. But such kindness necessarily causes the social situation to deteriorate because it breaks every social contract and enthrones Bartleby as a demigod among people who are not convinced of his merit to be one. The narrator discovers that saving Bartleby means sacrificing his own life, and he refuses to go this far, except for a brief moment, when he invites Bartleby to come into his home to live. In short, the narrator offers a more private setting for Bartleby's preferences. But Bartleby prefers not. He wishes to suffer the contradiction between his own desire to be a solitary individual and the desires felt by the other people living in his community. Bartleby, in effect, asks the narrator to sacrifice everyone and everything for his individuality. He requires a higher price than the narrator is willing to pay, and it is not certain that the price is sufficient to help Bartleby in any event.

Miller's reading focuses on the narrator's failure to be responsible for Bartleby. In order for me to be responsible for another person, Miller argues, I must be able to tell his or her complete life story. "How can I act responsibly toward a neighbor," he asks, "whose personality I do not know or whose story I do not know, or could not at least in principle come to know?" (144). Since prosopopoeia is necessary to tell a story, and the trope always reveals the failure of narrative, the narrator cannot ever come to know enough about Bartleby to act responsibly toward him. By definition, Bartleby is only a statue, a nonentity, and when the narrator tries to personify "it," he must necessarily fail, and so too must ethics fail. But a complete life story is not the key to ethical behavior, although ethics cannot exist in the absence of storytelling. If I could be responsible only for someone whom I knew absolutely, I could be responsible for no one, not even myself. This is why ethics substitutes for complete knowledge the concept of the "person." To be responsible for someone I need only to be able to tell the minimal narrative sufficient to designate him or her as a person. Thanks to this concept, I may depend on an emergency-room physician to save me from a gunshot wound without having to recount my life story beforehand, although the existence of the concept may not be sufficient to protect me from those who would try to shoot me.

This is why Miller stacks the deck when he defines Bartleby as a nonperson. "The divine injunction is," Miller explains, "to love your neighbor, but Bartleby is a ghost, a walking dead man, a living statue, a kind of zombie possessed by who knows what malicious spirit" (1990, 165). It is as if Ovid had made it clear that no metamorphosis took place in the story of Pygmalion. Pygmalion cavorts with a statue. He suffers from a deep and comic delusion. To see the tragedy in Ovid's story, however, we must be able to believe that Galatea comes to life. The same principle applies to "Bartleby the Scrivener." When Miller calls Bartleby a zombie, he rewrites a tragedy as a comedy, albeit a black one (to be precise, it is a variation on George Romero's *Night of the Living Dead*, in which the humans tolerate at their peril the zombies' hunger for human flesh out of a moral respect for their taste). The narrator's concern over his treatment of Bartleby becomes a joke. It is as silly as worrying about not being able to read every book in the world. But, in fact, Bartleby is a person in the narrator's eyes, and that makes all the difference. This personhood is the measure by which the narrator charts the disaster created both by his inability to treat Bartleby as a person and by the copyist's inability to act like one. Bartleby does come alive for the narrator, and he feels the ethical force of his failure to keep him alive at the end of the story, when he explains his friend's disposition as a consequence of witnessing the best intentions of humanity come to their undoing in the dead-letter office of the postal service. At this moment, the narrator understands that his experience with Bartleby has been analogous and that it might bring about a deadening of his own ability to be a person. His final exclamation, "Ah Bartleby! Ah humanity! " is an equation of despair drawn from his recognition that Bartleby and humanity have failed to take account of each other.

The narrator's words suggest a moral, commenting on the human condition and its best intentions. He recognizes that we may fail to stretch the concept of personhood sufficiently to include Bartleby and other eccentric personalities. But the failure does not lie in the concept. The fault lies in the failure of the specific narrative that makes up the concept in this particular case. (It is crucial to recognize as well that the failure of the narrative may in fact not be a failure at all because it does not go without saying that every person must sacrifice his or her life for any other person.) The narrator cannot tell himself the story necessary to make Bartleby into a person for whom he would sacrifice his own personhood, and he regrets the fact, even though it is not at all certain that he should.

"Bartleby the Scrivener" raises these ethical issues and others. If they are general formulations, they are only such because the particular themes of the story are themselves generalizable and because readers generalize them when they apply them to their own experience. Literary criticism as a genre pursues generalized reading to its most extreme expression, constructing "ideal readers" (or "sharp readers"), but it cannot really justify such readings because "ideal readers" do not have personal experiences, and they do not need moral counsel. Moral validity in interpretation takes place at the most personal levels, which is why the question of validity in interpretation is vertiginously complex for the ethics of reading. In sum, the ethics of reading exercises the greatest force in the most common experiences of reading. Perhaps, after reading Melville's story, a reader may be able to tell a different kind of story about the Bartleby in his or her own life. Perhaps not. The story does not depend on the education of a reader for its right to exist. But the story will not exist as an ethical experience if no reader ever takes this or another form of counsel from it, and to take counsel from the story, the reader must read for character.

The story of Pygmalion tells of an artist who brings a character to life. In the narrative version of the Pygmalion myth, if we accept Miller's reading, writers necessarily create characters who represent the failure of character. *What Maisie Knew*, for example, concludes when Maisie's understanding slips beyond the reach of the narrator and James himself. All narratives fail equally to join people in understanding because prosopopoeia cannot convey the necessary identifications. We might be tempted to accept this view if we saw literature as a prison house of narcissism, as Miller does. But how do we account for the equally weighty idea, expressed by Nietzsche, that artists do not create themselves in works of literature but create beyond themselves? From this point of view, that writer would be most fortunate who came to know before dying what his or her character knows. James would be lucky indeed to be able to say what Maisie knows. We would be lucky to be able to say what Maisie knows. All readers, including James, have difficulty saying what Maisie knows not because she does not know anything or because there is nothing to know but because they have been unlucky in their reading and because knowledge is difficult to possess. Perhaps they should take up the book again and read in the hope that knowledge will visit them.

The mysteries of personification upon which narrative depends require us to struggle with our identification with characters. No narrative could be seen as dangerous or redemptive if this were not the case. Maisie and Bartleby are not the embodiments of a moral. They do not present the pure moral vision of a narrator, author, or reader. Rather, Bartleby possesses the narrator. Maisie possesses James. Characters possess readers. When Maisie falls into a spasm and jerks, for example, trying to answer Mrs. Wix's questions, the narrative twitches and jerks. We fall into a spasm and jerk. It is certainly a popular idea that authors bring a character to the point of possessing their own moral knowledge, but if an author is lucky and the character remains a character, a power resides in what she or he knows. The difference between what Maisie knows and what James knows is paramount, and most important is what Maisie knows. Readers of the novel understand this fact. They spend all of their time trying to figure out what Maisie knew, not what James or a narrator tells them about her.

Reading for character is not popular among literary theorists. They associate it with the undergraduate experience of literature, and the majority oppose the idea that we might learn something from characters, while, paradoxically, they spend all their time with them. Part of Heidegger's legacy to contemporary thought, brought to literary criticism by Paul de Man and made into a method by Miller, is that the worst mistake we can make is to assume that art should contribute to ethics. This is why de Man redefined ethics in terms of "ethicity" (1979, 206), or the inhuman power of rhetoric, and why Miller has expended so much effort designing an ethics of reading in which ethics refers not to the chaotic passions and surprising virtues of human beings but to the undecidability of linguistic structure. But, sooner or later, the symbolism of this project must out. We will come to understand that a linguistic ethics cannot even describe what language is without hypothesizing about who people are and that its theory of language is really a metalanguage that fails at every instant to discover its true object (Siebers 1992, 21–35). Poststructuralism teaches that there is no metalanguage, but it ignores its own maxim. It is better to say that there is no metaethics. We invent strange ways of moving beyond character to talk about those apparent nonentities called *language, text,* and *book,* but these nonentities must become characters, if we are to say anything of value about ethical life. They, too, must be personified. Or, rather, we must realize that they are always already personifications.

Freud described the ethical itinerary of psychoanalysis with the phrase, "Wo Es war, soll Ich werden" (where it was, I must come to be). It is, in the end, another version of Pygmalion. The prosopopoeia refers to both Freud's metapsychology and the rule of kindness directing psychoanalytic therapy. Freud explained that the analyst must bring the patient to understand consciously where he or she has been unconsciously, thereby voyaging with the ego to the place of the id. His worst fear, however, which he felt most keenly in *The Ego and the Id*, was that in arriving in theory at its destination in the id, the ego might itself be said to have succumbed in practice to unconsciousness, to have been all along, in Freud's metaphor, only a rider living under the mistaken impression that he guides his horse where he wants to go, when, in fact, he goes only where the horse desires (1966–74, 19:25). Deconstruction is this nightmare. It describes the reader as a headless horseman riding a horseless horse. The horse is language, and it possesses even less horse sense than the id (the "it") described by Freud. The most "it" can do, to paraphrase de Man, is to engage in the headlong pursuit of noncomprehension, nonidentification, and nonmeaning (1984, 262).

In his therapeutic work, however, Freud resisted his worst fears. He hoped that patients might become healthy, become whole persons, through the act of telling stories about themselves and that they might arrive, as the result of this narrative experience, at a place where they would be able to accept what seemed to be a nonentity living within them as a person with whom they might live. They would find themselves by finding the other within themselves. They would learn, in short, to live with themselves and so be able to live with other people as well.

Reading brings authors, narrators, and readers to a place of otherness called character. "Where it was, I must come to be" is the moral of reading as much as there can ever be one. The "it" is not a nonentity, as Miller teaches, but the most radical expression of the third person or the person who is absent; but an identification between "I" and "it," between first and third persons, remains the most difficult task nevertheless. It is also the most worthwhile. Reading helps us to do this work. It initiates us into the mysteries of personification by which an "it" comes to be an "I," I bring a character to life, and characters bring me to life. Then only do I have a chance of possessing what I desire most. Then only might the "I" be rewritten as a "we," an end that provides the only truly satisfying closure for human beings in both narrative and life.

What Is There? A Dialogue on Obscenity, Sexuality, and the Sublime

Q: You suggested that we call this interview, "What Is There?" What is this all about? We are supposed to be talking about sexuality and the sublime, but I don't see the connection.

A: Sexuality and the sublime are, of course, fashionable topics today. They seem to be talked about in the same breath. In this sense, it is natural to bring them together. What I want to suggest, however, is that we don't have to work hard to bring them together, because they are already joined at the hip. The question "What is there?" is a heuristic device useful to uncover the hidden connections between sexuality and the sublime. It shows, first and foremost, that they are connected by the concept of obscenity. Modern thought is preoccupied with obscenity.

Q: Any time an academic mentions a word like *obscene*, you can be fairly sure that he or she is going to twist its meaning.

A: You're right, so let me pull out my hyphen fast and insert it. What I am calling the ob-scene is the preoccupation in modern and postmodern thought with the duplicity of interpretation, that any word, object, or subject may take additional or contradictory meaning from another context, another scene, an ob-scene, because of the force of desire. This mode of thought is most obviously derived from Freud and Heidegger, and a whole slew of terms conceals the same interpretive preoccupations: *indeterminacy, ideology, bad faith, kitsch, différance, uncanniness,* and so forth. The sublime fits here, and so does sexual desire, especially when it is used in the dynamic sense found in Lacan and others. In Foucault, for example, sex is the term that is and is not itself; otherwise he wouldn't be able to talk about the discourse of sex repressing sex.

I start with the question "What is there?" because it shows to what extent the marriage of Freudian psychoanalysis and Heideggerian existentialism is a facility of modern thought. Most philosophical exercises in the Continental tradition acknowledge and build upon their influence. What has not been acknowledged is that these exercises are ob-scene.

But I would say, in the final analysis, that the hyphen doesn't matter. There is something obscene in these kinds of philosophical exercises because they seem less concerned with meaning than desire. The effect is obvious in the palpable delight that people take in them, the sensual relish with which they finger the conundrums and their specific textual manifestations, and in the enjoyment they take in giving and taking away meaning.

The main question about obscenity concerns how, why, and whether what is there is obscene. This question can't be answered to anyone's satisfaction, however—and satisfaction is worth stressing here—because obscenity is about the sexual pleasure experienced in the giving and taking away of meaning. For example, obscenity is often described in terms of the attempt to denature the sexual act, to make it something else, something progressively different from what it should be. Vicissitudes of the instincts are pursued. Bodies are encrusted with fetishes. But, in fact, even the most common sexual act is viewed as obscene, as if seen through other eyes, when it is moved to a different context. Often the medium, whether written, plastic, or photographic, is held responsible for the obscenity, as if representation itself created the problem. Fredric Jameson, for example, goes so far as to say that "the visual is *essentially* pornographic" (1992, 1). This is an overreaction because it is not the presence of representation that makes sexual or other actions obscene. It is a matter of desire and its power to transform meanings and contexts. Obscenity appears when desire gets out of hand. Desire transforms actions, objects, and subjects, so that they are rendered beside themselves.

Q: Perhaps you had better run through this. It's fairly obvious that Continental philosophy owes a lot to Freud and Heidegger. But where does obscenity come into it?

A: Consider the question for a moment. "What is there?" is, first of all, a fundamental metaphysical question in the Heideggerian sense. Heidegger defines metaphysics as a desire for knowledge that exceeds the realm of physics and surpasses understanding as that mental faculty most concerned with the object world, thus setting into motion the faculty of pure reason. "What is there?" is a variation on the Heideggerian question "Why is there something rather than nothing?" insofar as it cuts to the grounds of questioning as an activity in order to expose those grounds as a possible abyss. Whence the double inflection of the question: "What is *there*?" means to ask about what lies there, fixed in time and space; "What *is* there?" also means "Nothing is there!" or "Why is there something rather than nothing?" since nothingness abounds. When we open our minds to this kind of question, Heidegger reports, "we cease to dwell in any of the familiar realms" (1961, 10).

A metaphysical question in the Heideggerian sense is also a sublime question because it exposes that the scene of the question, its ground *(Ur-grund),* is also another scene, an abyss *(Ab-grund).* Primary questions for Heidegger always spring from a ground but capture the essence of that ground, as if observing it from elsewhere. In the Kantian schema accepted by Heidegger, a lack in understanding is always filled by material taken from elsewhere, from the realm of reason. The sublime is this feeling of elsewhereness. It is the shadow cast by reason over what is there.

It would be a mistake, however, to forget that the sublime remains an affective category, which is simply to say that it identifies desires and feelings. How do we take account of a metaphysical feeling? How do we get from metaphysics back to physics? Where is the desire in metaphysical desire?

Now, I take it that a question defined as primary in the Heideggerian sense is also infantile in the Freudian sense. Staring into the abyss of the maternal absence, faced with the evidence of annihilation, little Martin Heidegger asks, "Why is there something rather than nothing?" The accent is on self-reference, of course, for the child's narcissism begs the question. His interpretation of the maternal something as the absence of the paternal something—as castration, to hang the usual name on it—gives primariness to his something, but, of course, he realizes in the bargain that he, too, might lose what he has there, and he is horrified.

Q: It's good you got that off your chest. Alienation and castration are hardly strange bedfellows these days. I suppose one could say that Lacan's greatest accomplishment was to allow us to see alienation in the mirror.

A: I'm not conflating Heidegger and Freud for the purpose of reducing metaphysics to an infantile body politic, although Heidegger's *Introduction to Metaphysics* is unquestionably "une métaphysique expliquée aux enfants" written by a man who desires ardently to be the father of a movement.

I want to find the common ground between sexuality and the sublime. This common ground, I think, lies in their scenic nature, by which I mean the tendency of desire to rely on the power of vision and to reproduce itself by transforming and multiplying scenes of affect. Desire is scenic. It relies on the creation of scenes, whether visible to the naked eye or imagined by the mind's eye. Sexual desire in both its animal and human forms is aroused by visual action *(Gestalt)*. Metaphysical desire is supposedly nonsexual, but it is tied to sexual desire insofar as it is concerned with the conditions of possibility not of what really exists but of what can be seen or imagined to exist—what exists in the realm of images. The sublime is metaphysical desire without an object. It is the experience of imagining what is there as if it led to or came from elsewhere.

Heideggerian metaphysics and Freudian sexuality focus on the same experience. It is an experience of desire deprived of its natural object, desire turned loose, turned obscene. Heidegger cannot ask what is there without "Being There," but if he were really there he would know what was there and would not need to ask the question. The question divides subject and object, revealing that they are each split in time and space, that each scene of selfhood or thingness is also another scene, that every scene has beside it another scene, an obscene. Nor can Freud's child ask the question without transforming what is fundamentally a question about self-reference and existential destiny into a question about sex. The question poses the twin destinies of every child—a destiny to question one's unique existence by way of anatomy, and a destiny to discover that anatomy is something other than existentially unique, that anatomy is fundamentally obscene in its ability to put one organ in the place of another.

In other words, modern reasoning in this mode always reaches the same impasse. This is why any question I might pose from its point of view is obscene: every question has a foundation from which the question both issues and escapes; every foundation is both a primal ground and an abyss. Such questions cannot be positioned anywhere near the site of their object. They are obscene because they look elsewhere for the object that is there. They desire always to be elsewhere, to lead what is there to somewhere else. They signify nothing other than this fact: the fact of obscenity. They are prayers to the gods of this fact. They are prayers to the gods of obscenity.

Q: I still don't have the sense that you are using the obscene in anything but the most eccentric usage. Let's try to get more concrete. Let's talk about some recent models of the sublime. I suppose Lyotard comes to mind.

A: Well, in Lyotard, the sublime and obscene are one, though he never says it openly. He rocks back and forth between Heidegger and Freud when convenient. But his description of modern alienation brings the two together. "The possibility of nothing happening is often associated with a feeling of anxiety," Lyotard explains, "a term with strong connotations in modern philosophies of existence and of the unconscious" (1991, 92).

It is this possibility that gives to abstract painting its sublime meaning. "Here and now there is this painting," Lyotard points out, "rather than nothing, and that's what is sublime" (1991, 93). The painting in question is by Barnett Newman, whose works Lyotard identifies with the modern aesthetic of the sublime. Newman's paintings supposedly present the unpresentable: the threat that nothing further will happen. The beholder stares at the apparatus, at what is there, into the paint and wonders, "Is it happening?" What is happening, of course, is nothing or everything—in any event, how is one to tell? According to Lyotard, it is not a matter of judgment anyway: the beholder renounces before the painting his or her selfhood, experiencing intense pleasure as the painting neutralizes the body and blocks up its drives. The beholder is fixed in blissful contemplation, whereas the painting is characterized by an excessive mobility. Thus the beholder finds a master, we might say, and throws himself or herself at its feet.

Q: I am not sure I'd want to go to a gallery with Lyotard.

A: I'm not overstating the masochism of the beholder. Lyotard calls the spectator a victim. I think there is an important intuition here, but it is wildly exaggerated.

Q: Doesn't Lyotard make the same point about abstract painting in "Acinema" (1989a)? The "apparatus" creates a scene from elsewhere, undoes the aesthetics of beauty, polarizes the mobility of the painting and the immobility of the beholder, and evokes intense feelings. One should recognize in this description the now-classic analysis of sublime subjectivity in which the subject's understanding is defeated by the object and he or she experiences intense pain and ecstatic self-awareness, but a self-awareness before an imagined power of reasoning far greater than his or her own.

A: This is only one part of it. The representational arts offer "two symmetrical examples" of what Lyotard calls "intensities." One is abstract painting, as you say. It is a matter of masochism. The other is the tableau vivant. Here the accent is on sadism and obscenity. Lyotard's example of the tableau vivant does not come from its classical roots, however, but from Sweden, where there exists a charming institution called the *posering*: "young girls rent their service to these special houses, services which consist of assuming, clothed or unclothed, the poses desired by the client" (1989a, 178). Lyotard does not use the word *obscene* to characterize the *posering;* he reserves this word for the Bride's body in Duchamp's *Large Glass.* But the notion of obscenity, another scene or a scene of elsewhereness, a detached region, is integral to the *posering:* "The object, the victim, the prostitute, takes the pose, offering his or her self as a detached region, but at the same time giving way and humiliating this whole person" (1989a, 178).

Q: What is obscene about the *posering* is the fact that the client commands the victim to be his object, and when the victim assumes the role of the object, his or her humiliation becomes a source of lively pleasure for the client.

A: You're beginning to anticipate. Lyotard doesn't put it that way. He is interested in the transgressive force of the *posering;* for him the obscenity is a plus. It's energy wasted for the pleasure of it. It's desire freed from production or reproduction. It's like lighting a match, as a child does, to look at the flame, instead of laying the match to a fuel and setting into motion some form of useful production.

Q: Lyotard's description of abstract painting leans toward the Heideggerian side, while that of the *posering* leans toward the Freudian side. Abstract painting, he says, relies on a peculiarly modern anxiety—the threat that nothingness abounds, which to call *anxiety* is already stacking the deck for his forthcoming libidinal analysis. The thrill of abstract painting is metaphysical; you have to be up on your Heidegger to enjoy this kind of painting. Without the taste for modern alienation, what effect would Newman's paintings have for Lyotard?

A: Lyotard nevertheless tries to root his analysis in the libidinal, to make the leap, via the term *anxiety,* from head to heart. Here is where his description grows unmistakably Sadean: the immobile and silent painting stands majestically before the impoverished spectator, whose anxiety feels very nice. The spectator sacrifices himself or herself to the master, who requires a victim to dominate.

Either abstract painting is a thematic rendering of modern alienation, where the threat of nothingness is enjoyable, or it is an allegory of sadomasochism. In any case, the feelings of powerlessness, of deprivation, and of loss are intimations of the sublime. Lyotard does not explain how this might be the case. Nor does he explain how modern alienation and sadomasochism relate: whether modern alienation seeks a solution in sadomasochism, whether these effects might be seen to block out each other.

Q: Lyotard's analysis is also tone-deaf as far as politics is concerned, despite the fact that politics is supposed to be his stock in trade.

A: Here Stanley Cavell is much more helpful and more political (1969). "Is it happening?" is indeed the question to ask about both abstract painting and pornography, but only because the threat of

What Is There?

fraud is so evident in both and not because we live in a world where nothing happens. Cavell explains that the beholder experiences a powerful skepticism before modern painting. It is, first, a skepticism about what Arthur Danto calls the "artworld." Is this art or fraud, the beholder wonders, and how would one know? Without reference to the artworld, the beholder is at a loss, and every time a beholder walks into a museum, he or she must accept on faith that the experts know what they are doing. Second, the beholder experiences a painful self-doubt or self-skepticism before the painting. The failure of the beholder's understanding to grasp the object makes him or her subservient to the superior reasoning of the expert; in short, the artworld embodies the sublime as a political institution. But because this sublime reasoning almost always manages to exceed the understanding of the beholder, he or she is in the position of posing the existential question, "Is it happening?" It means two things: "Is this art?" and "Have I arrived at the state of knowledge where I can recognize art and join the community of art experts?"

Q: What about the pornoworld? In my own brief but studious encounter with the pornographic cinema, I have noticed three obsessions: images of penetration; the money shot; and close-ups of the orgasmic female face. Whose obsessions are these? And what do they have to do with pleasure?

A: You're right to bring up the idea of a pornographic world, like the artworld. The same question poses itself to the beholder of pornography and to the beholder of abstract painting. Is it happening? Pornography is not about fantasy but about reality, since the beholder needs first to believe in the reality of the sexual act before he or she may begin to fantasize about it. The threat of fraud is very great in pornography because it shows desire actively transforming its objects. Suppose these people aren't really doing it. Suppose they aren't really enjoying it. What a scandal! Penetration shots show that the actors are at least being intimate. The so-called money shot, or male ejaculation, proves that he is enjoying it, since male anatomy does not permit an ejaculation without some pleasure. Finally, the orgasmic expression on a woman's face attempts to prove that she is enjoying it. Interestingly, this is the most difficult proof of all.

Q: Usually, when the actress is trying hardest to show she is enjoying herself, she is least successful. Often, verbalization is added: "Yes! Yes! It's happening!"

A: If you say so. You're the expert. It is obvious, however, that pleasure is defined in an entirely different way in pornography. There is a pornography world as much as an artworld. The staging of pleasure interferes with the pleasure of the actors. This is because their pleasure is not what is important. It is the pleasure of the beholder that matters. The actors sacrifice their pleasure to a superior imperative, doing what will please the audience not what pleases them. Their understanding of their own bodies is called into question, they experience displeasure, and imagine the existence of another scene—your television room or a movie house—where those for whom they act enjoy themselves.

Part of the phrasing of the question "Is it happening?" in the case of pornography, then, must include "Is it happening for me?" That is, "Are they doing it for me?" What is common to the *posering* and to the pornographic cinema is the feeling that must come over the clients when they recognize that the actors are actively trying to fulfill their desires, to give them what they want, even though it is not what the actors want. This is obscene because the actors are operating on another scene where they are objects of a point of view, to which they beckon, rather than being objects for one another, and because the clients are operating on another scene where they possess a point of view superior to their actual reality and are beckoned to.

Q: In one analysis of sublimity, which exists everywhere today, the pleasure in these situations—abstract painting, the *posering*, pornography—would be ascribed to the feelings of power experienced by subjects.

A: I think this analysis is incomplete because, at least in the case of pornography, the subject matter is sexual. The immediate point of importance here, however, is that the effects of these situations rely not on the metaphysical condition of modernity and the threat of nothingness to it—which is a wholly apolitical formulation—but on something like a specific world—an artworld, a pornoworld—having a limited political structure. There are surely experiences of sublimity that are transcendental, usually of a religious nature, but the specific cases of sublimity here are more narrow. That is what distinguishes the modern and the classical sublime. The modern sublime differs from the classical sublime in significant and easily registered ways: the failure of understanding of the subject is extremely local (she is in a museum and does not understand the paintings); the subject places herself in willing tutelage to a highly visible institution (she goes to the gift shop and buys a book on modern art); and the sublime intelligence, holder of pure reason so to speak, is in fact presentable and nameable, being often associated with the institution or its representatives (the book is by Jean-François Lyotard).

Q: This is to say that the "Is it happening?" has a very specific and appreciable context, having to do with the condition of knowledge of the subject.

A: I think so. It's politics, cultural, sexual, or otherwise.

Q: A moment ago, you said something about the importance of sex in pornography.

A: It has to be important. I find things rather confusing in analyses of pleasure today. On the one hand, situations of obvious sexual content are said to be pleasurable because of power relations. On the other hand, we live in a psychoanalytic culture in which everything gets reduced to sex. The sublime has been used in some ways to stop sexual interpretation. It doesn't succeed because it eroticizes defects of understanding as sexual masochism. But these days, it is far better to see identity as erotic than the sexual act.

A return to the language of instinct would be one way to straighten out the confusion, but "instinct" is a forbidden term today. It started with Lacan's revision of Freud. Lacanian psychoanalysis is based on the nature-culture split, taken most immediately from Lévi-Strauss but inherent in Freud's idea that the neuroses derive from nonorganic causes, that is, culture and its discontents. According to Lacan's theory of the drives, instincts are natural and the drives are cultural and fallen. Animal instincts fire on cue, but humans replace instinctual cues with purely artificial ones, with symbols, making their instincts misfire. Thus desire originates when symbols interfere with instinct. This is what Lacan's "Mirror Stage" (1977) is all about. It is also what makes obscenity possible.

Q: There is an obvious courting of sublime aesthetics on the current scene. You'd think that instinct would be part of it. What could be more sublime than instinct? It describes a situation in which the subject finds himself or herself in the grip of a powerful force that strains understanding.

A: The discourse of the drives is really an undoing of the sublime, if we define the sublime as an order wholly foreign to human understanding. It tries to render the sublime in cultural terms, as power relations, as narrative sequences, as linguistic orders that occur in the social world.

Freud's Wolf Man case history is interesting in this regard and paradigmatic of modern trends. Freud spends considerable effort trying to explain why his patient finds a washerwoman erotic. The Wolf Man comes upon a maid washing the floor. She is bent over on all fours, her buttocks projecting, scrubbing away at the floorboards. Now, one doesn't need a theory of family romance to explain the eroticism of this posture. Nevertheless, Freud makes up a narrative to account for

The Subject and Other Subjects

the attraction. He argues the case that the washerwoman's pose reminds the Wolf Man of his mother's posture in an intercourse *a tergo* in the primal scene. The erotic content of the washerwoman's posture derives from the primal scene. It has no erotic content of its own. This is the theory of the drives in its purest expression. The sexuality is symbolic.

I don't think the Wolf Man's problem was that he found this posture attractive. His problem was that he was so overwhelmed by his sexual instincts that he could not align them properly with the symbolism of social existence. Whenever he saw a woman assume this posture, he fell violently in love with her.

Q: You begin to sound like Camille Paglia.

A: I have only one thing to say about Camille Paglia. Susan Sontag is smarter.

Q: I came across something in *Cosmopolitan* magazine not too long ago (Kurtz 1993). A woman wrote a letter to an advice column. Here is the story. It seems that the woman goes with her husband to a benefit party, where as a gimmick the men dress in drag and serve drinks to the ladies. When they get home, they make passionate love, the best in ten years of marriage. Soon the husband begins to change into her clothes the minute he gets home from work. He asks her to tie him to a chair in the basement. She does it, and when she stands back to look at him, she has an orgasm. She buys a pair of patent leather pants, which she wears when she trains her slave, whom she has renamed Barbra. But she is getting concerned. "What's happening to us?" she asks. "Are we headed for serious trouble?"

A: So what advice do they get?

Q: The columnist tells them to enjoy themselves, not to worry, that their sexual fantasies are perfectly matched. "Aren't you sorry," she says, "that you didn't let it all out sooner?"

A: I suppose this might prove that power is sexy. Maybe it is. But what interests me about this story, presuming it was not written by the staff at *Cosmo,* is that the emotions felt by the couple are contaminated by ethical considerations. Why is the woman worried about what is happening? If all she were after was pure pleasure, she would be satisfied. But her emotions are startled as much by an ethical shock as a sexual one.

I think the advice columnist does the woman a disservice by dismissing her ethical concern about her conduct. It can't be separated from the sexual pleasure. It obviously contributes to the pleasure in some cases, while it acts as an obstacle in others. In any case, the affect of the sexual experience is mixed with a moral sensibility.

What Is There?

Q: You're saying that the pleasure of the scene is transgressive.

A: No, I don't think so. Both the pleasure and displeasure of the situation depend on the appearance of someone on the scene. It is about the characters they are playing, and characters are not merely roles. They are also a form of morality. These people are enjoying themselves, but they are afraid of what they are becoming. It stands to reason that what they are becoming is part of the pleasure.

When Heidegger or Lyotard say there is something rather than nothing, it means something. What is there is important. Newman, for example, gives an interpretation of his own painting that Lyotard dismisses. Newman says that what is there procures "personality" by revealing itself instantaneously. Lyotard calls the idea unfortunate, since he doesn't believe that personality is at stake. But personality is very much at stake. This is because these sublime affects occur aesthetically by way of the ethical.

Take the case of the *posering* again. There is the client and the sex worker. She poses for the client. Why is she doing it? She is doing it because *(a)* of the money, *(b)* she likes it, *(c)* she was abused as a child, *(d)* she's stupid, *(e)* she's a prostitute, *(f)* she's a nympho, *(g)* she's a bitch, *(h)* she's a slut, *(i)* she's a whore—all the way to *z*. Some of these reasons make sense. Others are obscene phantasms. What difference does it make? It makes all the difference or no difference. It makes all the difference because her reasons and past actions determine her character, and this character matters to her. It makes no difference because certain actions obscure a broad view of character, and in most cultures, sex is one of these marked actions.

So for whatever reason she acts, her action contributes to both the client's and our idea of her character. Let's say she is doing it for the money—the most obvious reason. Why has she chosen to do this for a living? Why is it more bearable than working in a chicken factory, for example? Because *a, b, c . . . z*. Her act, which is not an exposure of her entire personhood, comes to personify her character as such. In her private personhood, she may have integrity, but once she engages in a marked action, it becomes extremely difficult for her to represent her integrity to other people. She is personified as a certain kind of character.

Q: But it is in the client's interest not to think about her real motivations. He doesn't want to know that she is doing it for the money.

A: He knows she is doing it for the money. Tell the client. What does it change? He will think, "Well, I've always fantasized about a woman who would do anything for money." Aren't the patented obscenities of sexual ecstasy, the insults that flow from his lips when

The Subject and Other Subjects

he is aroused, a fairly accurate expression of the character she assumes when she goes to work? Isn't it important for her to personify this moral character if her work is to be successful? She can't control her own representation. Nor can the client for that matter. He hasn't invented the game. He doesn't choose his arousal. It happens to both of them, which is not to say that they are innocents.

Q: This ethos of sadomasochistic play has analogues in modern theory. In his early work, Foucault identifies the ethical dilemmas posed by violence and exclusionary practices, indicating how difficult it is to avoid them in the social world. But in *The History of Sexuality*, he finds an escape from such dilemmas in the eroticism of sadomasochistic theater, where discipline brings pleasure, and warnings about violence are replaced by concerns about who gets penetrated in the sexual act. There is a little book in the Foucauldian style by John Rajchman called *Truth and Eros* (1991). The cover illustration embellishes upon what Foucault's new erotics mean by reproducing a Roman painting called *Donna flagellata e baccante danzante*, which pictures a beating accompanied by music and dancing.

A: Foucault's new erotics fail as an ethics because they ignore the central moral dilemma of sadomasochistic play: whether people harm themselves by pleasing people who find pleasure in being hurt. This is why the woman writes to *Cosmo* magazine. She is worried that her sexual practices will change her morally.

Q: In fact, the columnist tells her that her husband will tell her when she goes too far, when it really hurts.

A: Of course. This is because the columnist is on the husband's side. She isn't worried about what it might do to the woman to envision herself as a torturer. But I think the woman is most worried about this image.

Q: What current theories of the sublime miss in matters sexual is the appearance of images such as these. They claim that the sublime is about the unpresentable . . .

A: The classical sublime is. It is about something in the present— what remains always in the present and cannot be dragged by thought into history, into the past or the future, cannot be viewed in terms of either origin or goal. It is the burning bush that is not transformed by its own burning.

Q: But there are presences in the sexual sublime and in the artistic sublime, for that matter. Call them objects or subjects, but they are there. They may be undecidable and so forth, but they embody a problem, a decision of some kind, and they offer it for our contemplation.

They are objects represented on one scene and another scene at the same time.

A: This is why I say that the sublime today is really about beauty. Beauty occurs when all of the issues of interpretation are directed at an object. It doesn't matter if the object is ambiguous. In fact, a certain view of aesthetics has always claimed that objects must be ambiguous to be beautiful. The classical sublime can't be embodied in an object. Remember what Kant says. There is no more sublime passage in the Jewish Law than the commandment: "Thou shalt not make unto thee any graven image, or any likeness of any thing that is in heaven or on earth, or under the earth" (1952, §29).

Q: Personally, I find Rothko and Pollock to be very beautiful—Newman, of course, less so. There is an old *New Yorker* cartoon. It shows a couple, sitting on the deck of their very modernist beach house, staring out at the sunset. The sun is rectangular and made up of three horizontal bands of color—a painting à la Mark Rothko. The caption is: "Now, there's a nice contemporary sunset!"

A: Sunsets are said to be beautiful, aren't they? You say it's a couple looking at the sunset?

Q: Yes, they're wearing sunglasses and having cocktails.

A: I find that to be significant. First, the kinds of emotions usually described as sublime are not apt to be shared. Second, what does it mean for a couple to have an object in common? This kind of connection has always been associated with beauty, and it means something when it is associated with sexual difference, however muted. That the family romance has the ability to surmount sexual difference places it at the nucleus of the political romance, whose utopian ideal is, after all, to create a life in common in spite of the stubborn differences separating people. What could be more stubborn than sexual difference? And yet there is very little thought on the current scene that links sexual union to beauty.

Portia Williams Weiskel, the wife of Thomas Weiskel, who drowned tragically while skating with their daughter, is one of the few exceptions. She is by virtue of her grief a true critic of the sublime in the most active sense when she writes in the personal introduction to her dead husband's work: "It is a relentless horror for me that he and our daughter are not with us. But he used to the full his twenty-nine years and he died as he lived—brave, loving, vulnerable, and with flourish" (1976, xv). She understands that a beauty resides in the family romance and that Thomas Weiskel becomes a figure of the sublime when death tears him from her. Virility is a trope of the sublime in the

The Subject and Other Subjects

West because of the potential absence of men from that romance, because of the ease with which men have been torn throughout history from their loved ones by the many natural and cultural forces of violence. Virility is nothing other than the willingness to sacrifice oneself to danger in the attempt to preserve the romance of family or community.

Q: Since you bring up sexual difference, let's talk about feminism for a moment.

A: It's hard not to, when you bring the sublime and sexuality together.

I'm not sure it comes down to feminism, however. The fact that sexuality and the sublime seem to orbit around what I've been calling obscenity wasn't caused by the advent of feminism. Probably, it's the other way around. Feminism became viable as a discourse because our moral and aesthetic ideas are so caught up with obscenity. One way to visualize the modern sublime is to see it as the psychological point of view of a subject whom another subject is trying to represent as beautiful. All of the desire of one subject is directed at another. It makes a call upon this subject in the name of beauty to be the object of reality around which these desires might collect. But the beautiful object supposedly responsible for the emergence of these desires experiences herself as a fraud. I say "herself" because historically woman has found herself in this obscene situation. The man sees the beauty there. The woman, who is what is there, feels only the force of the desire and its call upon her to embody this desire and to reflect it back to the man. She feels possessed. All of these forces—instinctual, social, political, ethical—compel her into the character, despite the fact that she knows that she is not "beautiful." She experiences a failure of understanding about her own self as the object.

The feminist critique of beauty is an attempt to explain the beauty of the object through other sources and logics and thereby to repair the defect in understanding. These sources and logics have various names: patriarchy, history, ideology, male violence, and so forth. The problem is that they are sublime constructions in the classical sense and cannot be presented on any scene. There is no secret club for the instruction of patriarchy. It is not a political institution in the real sense of the term. If it is not there, somewhere, how do you go about changing it?

Q: You're not saying that sexism doesn't exist? It's very apparent.

A: No, sexism exists, obviously, because there are individuals who experience and reject the call upon them to be a certain sexual way, and these responses contribute to history and to public understanding.

What Is There?

All I am saying is that the institutionalization of sexism is hard to deal with because it is not locatable. There is always a gap between individual conduct and sexism as an institution. When a man is accused of sexist behavior, for example, he is made the object of a criticism, but he may experience a lack of identity between who he conceives himself to be and the role associated with him by the criticism. He embodies the inside point of view: he is skeptical that his self could be responsible for all the effects being ascribed to it.

You know there is a famous example of bad faith developed by Sartre (1966, 96–98). It strikes one as very sexist now. He says that woman is by nature divided in two: she is her self and her body.

A woman goes on a date with a man for the first time. He pays her a compliment, says she is attractive. She accepts the compliment and thinks him very polite, very nice. The man takes her hand. She leaves it there. According to Sartre, it is there and not there from her point of view, because she is duping herself over the gesture, trying to make it into a measure of esteem and not eroticism. He says the woman is in bad faith because she doesn't know what she wants. She is profoundly aware of the desire that she inspires, but naked desire would humiliate her, Sartre explains, so she pretends it is not there. Yet she would not be satisfied with pure respect, devoid of sexual attraction. She wants to be desired. What she wants, Sartre goes on, is a feeling addressed wholly to her "personality"—to her full freedom as a human being—and yet, contradictorily, this feeling must also express a desire to possess her body.

Q: For Sartre, of course, the man's gestures are not in bad faith.

A: No, at least he never says so. The woman is the example of bad faith.

The point to make is that the woman's bad faith has a sexual content. Perhaps the essence of sexism is this accusation, to say that women don't know what they want, that they mean "yes" when they say "no"—as if this kind of dilemma applied only to women as a sex and not to all human beings.

Today feminism applies the idea of bad faith to male behavior in terms of power. It introduces a crisis of male desire over its bad faith. It says to men, "You pretend to be interested in sex, but you are really interested in power," just as Sartre said earlier, in a manner of speaking, to feminists—the women who want their full freedom recognized—"You pretend to be interested in freedom, but you are really interested in sex."

Q: So this is why some people say women have all the power in sexual relations, while others say men have it? Because both insights are spoken from the interior consciousness of the object; both see what is being done to them on the other side and experience it as powerlessness.

A: What is sexist is the asymmetry of the objectification. Women are represented as sex objects, and men are accused of harming them by making them play this role. Men are represented as having the power to make sex objects, and women are accused of harming them by making them play this role. There will never be anything like true sexual equality until women begin to worry that their sexual desires might hurt men, and men begin to worry that ascribing power to women might cause them harm.

But it is unlikely that this will happen for some time. It seems laughable, for instance, to say that female desire might debase men. As for power, male and female power are considered different animals.

Q: Some of what you have been saying reminds me of the anamorphic gaze, the psychoanalytic notion of traumatic vision, in which nothing begets something—the *objet petit a* as a principle of the gaze, where the object seen is both the object-cause of desire and the object posited by desire.

A: Lacan's ideas are very much in the mold I have been discussing. His theory is a blend of Heideggerian thought—derived from Sartre—and Freud. But I think he is right to see the common ground between sexuality and sublimity in the visual. Invisible agents such as scents or sounds may stimulate desire, but they are successful only if they embody an object on a scene, acting like Proust's madeleine to summon images.

Q: Actually, I was thinking of Slavoj Žižek, whose work is all the rage now. He works on matters sexual and ideological, integrating psychoanalytic theory and popular culture. His book *Looking Awry* (1991) touches upon obscenity in terms of the Lacanian gaze. He analyzes various situations where two realities interpose themselves, or at least where one has the impression of two realities or two substances coinciding. The situation is one where the gaze becomes puzzled by desire, or vice versa, because Žižek gives two readings. This is his first reading: if we look straight on at something, we see it as it is, we see what is there. But if our gaze is troubled by desire, we look awry and we get a blurred image. Then there is a second reading, which he seems to prefer: if we look at a thing straight on, objectively, we see nothing but a formless blot. The object presents distinctive features, becomes something, only if we look at it awry, with a view distorted by desire or anxiety. The latter is the *objet petit a*, because the object is objectively nothing; it is something begot from nothing.

"Desire," Žižek claims, "'takes off' when 'something' (its object-cause) embodies, gives positive existence to its 'nothing,' its void" (1991, 12).

A: For Žižek, there is something rather than nothing because we desire there to be. Culture is there. Culture is desire. So the look awry sees what is there. But what does Mr. Žižek see? He sees nothing. Why? Because his eyes are undimmed by desire. How does he manage it?

This shows the naturalist fallacy in Žižek and Lacanian theory: the image is the instinctive pattern turned awry (put into the mirror), a fall from nature into culture. But the question "Why is there something rather than nothing?" is asked from a perspective before the fall and tries to recoup this point of view, what I might call the zero point from which desire takes off. The psychoanalyst is the only one who possesses the simultaneous view of the two objects, the two realities, the two substances, nothing and something—whatever terms you prefer. But it is clear that a narrative exists that traces the path of desire from a point of departure connected with an object whose reality is uncontaminated by desire, whose existence is pure, like Kant's thing-in-itself. The Lacanian analyst always tries to locate the zero point of desire, the no thing to which desire is added.

Q: Žižek says, following Lacan, that the coincidence of the two realities in the gaze defines the position of the pervert. He says that the pervert's gaze overlaps with the gaze with which God looks at himself.

A: This is one way to define the obscene, although it strikes me as a bit loony. Why would God be looking at himself?

Here we begin to approach, however, what modern philosophical exercises in obscenity share with sexual obscenity. Žižek has an amusing penchant for jokes and punch lines that turn situations inside out in an instant. I would compare this penchant to the general fondness for loony formulas found in psychoanalysis. This fondness is not so innocent, however, and Žižek's stories are very telling about his brand of psychoanalysis. For example, he recounts the farcical story about the analyst whose patient complains that there is a crocodile under his bed (1991, 80). The analyst shrugs it off as a hallucination. Shortly afterward, the patient stops coming to sessions, and the analyst assumes he has been cured. Then the analyst runs into a mutual friend and asks how the former patient is doing. "To whom are you referring?" the friend replies. "The one who was eaten by a crocodile?"

It is clear that Žižek is not an analyst in this mode. He is an analyst who believes in crocodiles. His readings of films and popular cul-

The Subject and Other Subjects

ture show this fact consistently. Consider his interpretations of Steven Spielberg's *Empire of the Sun* and Terry Gilliam's *Brazil* (1991, 172 n. 10). In both, it would seem, the hero identifies with a fantasy creation. Jamie, the boy in Spielberg's film, is fascinated by airplanes and longs to fly one. The hero of *Brazil* fantasizes that he is a giant butterfly. Žižek turns the stories inside out. He says that *Empire of the Sun* is about an airplane dreaming about being Jamie, while *Brazil* tells the story of a giant butterfly fantasizing that he is a human bureaucrat. This is what I mean by loony formulas. It is a mode of thinking that tries to imagine the impossible perspective of an object, to which desire is then hyperbolically added.

Q: So what is most readable is really unreadable, and vice versa. Žižek claims that Kafka is so readable only because of his excessive unreadability. Joyce is unreadable because so many readings of his work can be imagined.

A: I would say, rather, that it is less a question of interpretation than of a tendency to reduce everything to an inanimate state, to a statue, for one's own perverse enjoyment. It is a form of obscene thinking because it establishes the reality of something living as something dead. The analyst makes nothing begetting something the standard formula and then traces the emergence of desire, the dream of coming to life, from nothing to something, as if it could happen only under his or her gaze. After all, the analyst is the only one to see the true state of things. The vision is perverse. It brings everything back to the obscene object, which only the analyst can see because the unconscious speaks through him or her.

Q: Well, Žižek calls the central impossibility around which every signifying network is structured the obscene object, but I don't see that it is really obscene as such.

A: It is obscene as such. Who is the sadist? The sexual sadist is an aesthete of the sublime. Lacan himself argues that the sadist occupies the position of the object-instrument manipulated by some radically heterogeneous will. What could this be other than the unconscious? The analyst is in the position of the sadist because his or her pleasure is to tell the story of this tyrannical and incomprehensible will, without being able to understand it. So the formula is not so loony after all. It is rather terrifying. But look at how powerful it is! Under the obscene gaze of the sadist, the mouth open in pain becomes an organ of delight, cries of anguish become groans of enjoyment; under the interrogation of the sadist, little boys confess that they are only airplanes dreaming of becoming human beings, tormented office workers say they are giant butterflies and plead to lead one day the life of a bureaucrat. The sadist sees the world as dross, which upon his touch turns into gold. The sadist does not fear that the beautiful, golden things of the world will turn into gifts of excrement. He has the Midas touch. He envisions the pit of shit in the Inferno as Dante's shining world.

Q: Someone with the Midas touch is not interested in finding gold, in touching gold. I begin to think that you are someone who is interested in beauty.

A: I wouldn't want the Midas touch, if that is what you mean.

Q: Midas was a miser, but, more important, he was by necessity a misanthrope. He did not know beauty because his world was too dangerous for anyone else to share. He had nothing in common with anyone, one might say, with the stress on the common, because everything common soon became in his hands uncommon.

A: Beauty is what we have in common. This is its interest for aesthetics as well as politics. The advocates of the modern sublime are in flight from beauty because they distrust most what beauty represents, a life in common and its travails—all the earnest graspings after consensus that characterize politics, aesthetics, and sexual love. Beauty is a form of deep mystification, apparently, and we are better off without it. It always leads to trouble, to world war, for example. Better to lead a life undeluded, where we face up to the full horror and violence of life, which includes, of course, everything, especially what doesn't seem horrible at first glance. Then we will not be tricked by life.

The modern sublime names the affective realm of this horror, this fear of being tricked by life, and it presents itself as an advance in knowledge about the human condition. But, in fact, it gives no knowledge about horror or humanity or anything else because it has no object. It is a preference for nothing rather than something, for unconscious agreement over conscious agreement, a preference to name what we have in common as anything other than what we might create. What we have in common is metaphysical Being, perhaps, or it is the unconscious—in any case, it is not a matter of human creation and responsibility.

Q: But not everyone is unconscious, despite the fact that unconsciousness is so all-embracing. The experts know what we agree about unconsciously; they know what the sublime represents, and they will not fail to tell us. Nor will they fail to tell us that they know more than we, that they know what we need.

A: This is why the modern sublime also names the affective realm of modern terrorist politics and bureaucracy, the realm of all the petty and not-so-petty dictators who speak to us in the name of a higher purpose, who ask us to sacrifice our freedom, as they say they have, to a sublime cause, even though it is incomprehensible to us. It is the only way, they say, to change what is common and dirty and decadent into something extraordinary, golden, and glorious. It is the only way to become great. This greatness will not last forever, of course—only small people want that kind of greatness—but it will feel pretty good. It is the kind of greatness that will burn us out in a blaze of glory. Heidegger speaks this way about Being and the fate of Europe under National Socialism, for instance. He disdains anything less than full disclosure of Being, and it has to happen with a bang. "What is great," he sermonizes about the philosophy of Being, "can only begin great. Its beginning is in fact the greatest thing of all. A small beginning belongs only to the small, whose dubious greatness it is to diminish all things; small are the beginnings of decay, though it may later become great in the sense of the enormity of total annihilation" (1961, 13).

Q: The beautiful is something small.

A: It begins small and it stays small. It is a very human thing. It is as difficult to possess as the sublime, but it is worth having.

So there you have it.

Q: Have what? What is there?

A: Beauty is there. Right there.

Q: There, there, now.

Politics and Peace

> To Perpetual Peace. Whether this satirical inscription on a certain Dutch shopkeeper's sign, on which a graveyard was painted, holds for *men* in general, or especially for heads of state who can never get enough of war, or perhaps only for the philosophers who dream this sweet dream, is not for us to decide. However, the author of this essay does set out one condition. . . . The practical politician must not claim, in the event of a dispute with a theorist, to detect some danger to the nation in those views that the political theorist expresses openly and without ulterior motive. . . . By this *clausula salvatoria*, the author of this essay will regard himself to be expressly protected in the best way possible from all malicious interpretation.
> —Immanuel Kant, preface to *Perpetual Peace*

My goal is to work my way back to Kant's defensive preface to *Perpetual Peace,* the prophetic essay situated by many at the origin of modern conceptions of peace and international diplomacy. Suffice it to say for the moment that the following reflections are intended to reveal the epitaph in Kant's epigraph—the eternal repose residing in perpetual peace.

Imagining Relation

One of the master ideas to come down to us from the eighteenth century holds that the imagination is central to all relations between self and other, however one might designate this otherness. The imagination is central to Adam Smith's idea of sympathy, and Kant uses it as a bridge to unify his critical philosophy. Whether referring to objects or other people, we require a faculty by which to extend understanding to them, and this faculty continues even today to be described as imaginative. Postmodern theorists, for example, conceive of human relations in terms of identity politics, but at the core of identification is the power to imagine, be it the power to sympathize or to conceive of a party different from oneself. In effect, then, relation is itself a function of the imagination. Moreover, no relation, I want to claim, exists for long that cannot be well imagined, for which some symbolic object or idea cannot be found.

The four dominant modes of relation are religion, aesthetics, ethics, and politics.[1] They deserve to be called modes insofar as they name different others to which the self (or another principal) may relate imaginatively. Religion is about the relation of goodness between subject and god called the sublime. Often nature, fate, or providence as personified forces or overarching systems are also called sublime. Aesthetics is about the relation of goodness between subject and object called beauty. Ethics is about the relation of goodness between subjects called character or virtue. Finally, politics is about the relation of goodness between communities called peace.

Peace may seem at first glance to be an odd choice to name the relation of goodness in politics. A more obvious candidate might be the idea of utopia. But utopia comes into being as a concept only with Thomas More's treatise in 1516, and this late invention seems to exclude its being considered as the privileged good of politics. More important, the traditional opposition between ethics and politics exposes the unfitness of utopia as a candidate for the political good. Ethics and politics are often at war because the ethical imagination at its purest does not want to sacrifice even one person to improve the relations between other people. Ethics strives for a wholly inclusive community, but it defines this community as a collection of autonomous individuals having value in themselves only as ends and never as means to an end. If ethics aims at a wholly inclusive community of individuals, then, utopia may be described by rights as an ethical concept, regardless of the fact that utopian desire seems to stress the wrong perspective on this community, coming as it does from the collective rather than the individual point of view. The ethical dimension of the utopian is made obvious by the realization that a utopia can never be considered as a truly good place until it is the only place. For a utopia based on exclusion is no utopia at all.

Only if we begin to imagine politics as a relation occurring

---

1. I will not discuss cognition, although it is surely dominant, because its objects are various, whereas the modes of relation of interest to me here tend to represent their objects as being of a certain kind.

between communities, might we understand that peace is the political good. That is to say, in my definition, politics concerns how relations are to be established and maintained between more than one political group. This definition has the advantage of trying to name a realm in which the relation between principal (self) and other is noticeably different from those of ethics, aesthetics, and religion. It also recognizes that the primary difficulty of politics lies not in forming communities, which in fact spring forth spontaneously, but in finding ways of harmonizing the needs of different communities. This difficulty applies obviously to factions within one society as much as to different nation states, although I will be most concerned with the latter.

I recognize that my definition may seem extreme or restrictive, especially given the current scene in which one is hard put to see how anything might *not* be defined as political. Why am I adopting such a restrictive definition? For two reasons. First, I am engaging in a thought experiment about the act of definition itself. How do we represent the limits of definition? What relations and connections do we need to imagine, and how, to distinguish one object from another—which is, after all, what definition is all about? Finally, how do we define the relations used to represent definitions? Second, I want to express my gratitude to Kant, whose method of thinking I find increasingly appealing. Kant sketched fairly strict definitions of all the modes discussed here with the exception of politics. This might have been the case because he was so intent on understanding the individual nature of thought that he did not focus on its collective dimension. But it might also have been the case because politics has subjects and objects so different from those of the other modes of relation that it endangers the imagination of relation as such.

Kant's central thrust, it seems to me, is always aesthetic, that is, based on individual feeling.[2] He focuses on the beauty of thinking about how objects come to symbolize our thoughts and emotions, usually our moral ones, emphasizing the process by which the relation between self and other is itself represented. But Kant is also obsessed with what I would call the problem of death-defying objectivity, being well aware of the potential rigor mortis of thought embodied in objects. Understanding requires a real or symbolic object, Kant holds,

---

2. This statement may seem jarring to those who consider Kant's greatest achievements to be in moral philosophy. Nevertheless, the moral self emerges in Kant via what can only be called an aesthetic process, and aesthetics remains the primary mode by which the individuality of the moral self is represented both to itself and to others. See Luc Ferry (1993) for a discussion of how subjectivity became an aesthetic function.

if understanding is to be put in relation, if it is to have any consequence, if it is to lead us toward the world and away from death. But anytime that understanding comes to reside in an object, it risks objectification; it risks to die on the spot, losing the imaginative and creative flexibility that we like to associate with it. To take Kant's most famous example of this paradox, freedom is incomprehensible precisely because it cannot be objectively represented. Freedom remains freedom only as long as it bears no relation to anything else.

Kant makes a crucial advance in our understanding of the limits of political representation when he discovers the inability of individuals to understand freedom. It is true that he defines this limitation as a problem of cognition rather than imagination: that is, since cognition cannot relate to metaphysical objects such as freedom in its own terms, it requires a leap of faith via the imagination to conceptualize a mode of relation beyond itself. But what if a similar limitation arises in the case of political imagination? What if individual thought fails to provide an objective representation of community? This would mean that Kant's remarks about freedom—which is after all the concept charged in his philosophy with bearing the weight of individuality relative to the requirements of social existence—are in fact a confession that human beings cannot imagine the political relation at all.

This observation, if correct, requires two additional comments, one by way of nuancing Kant's definition of politics and another by way of anticipating my eventual return to *Perpetual Peace* and the graveyard with which it begins. First, Kant defines freedom on the basis of autonomy and against heteronomy, which means that freedom is attached to individuality in itself and not to anything remotely resembling interpersonal or social relations. Freedom is, quite simply, the defining quality of the individual self. However, if human beings cannot adequately comprehend their own individual freedom, consider how difficult it is for them to imagine free relations between two or more political communities. Second, if political relation exists at the limits of the human imagination, it explains why Kant begins *Perpetual Peace* with a reference to death: in the absence of a mode of symbolizing what the political is, he has no choice but to symbolize this absence itself. Thus, eternal rest, the death of all human relating, comes to stand for perpetual peace, the relation of the good for politics.

Incidentally, Kant's most gifted interpreters—I am thinking here especially of Hannah Arendt and the existentialists[3]—have tried to

---

3. See especially Hannah Arendt (1982), where she translates Kant's idea of judgment into political terms. In terms of the existentialists, I am thinking about their

repair this gap in the political imagination by defining politics on the basis of individual acts of self-reflection. The result has been a description of politics in which the individual creates his or her own political identity through an act of self-imagination, the successful community being one lucky enough to contain many of these self-imaginers. I am not convinced that this is a bad approach, especially since it has inspired some of my own work, but my goal here is obviously to experiment with another perspective, one that tries to define the political in terms of a distinct and unique relation recognizably different from those of aesthetics, ethics, and religion.

It might be objected that we reach an impasse whenever we try to imagine a relation and that it hardly makes sense to focus in particular on the aporias of the political imagination. It is now commonplace in deconstructive circles to argue that relation necessarily involves the illegal transport of thought from one term to another, since the simple fact of relation is always based on a referential error.[4] Nevertheless, we do imagine relations all the time, so I consider it a groundless philosophical worry to fret for too long about how the facticity of relation might impede more pragmatic thoughts about *kinds* of relations. Here one of Stanley Cavell's analogies might clarify what I mean: the fact that I have a body is not the same kind of fact as the fact that I have a body of such and such a size in such and such a condition. "We are not well advised," Cavell muses, "to inspect the population to discover who among us in fact have bodies and who have not" (1994, 7). In other words, the fact that we imagine relations is a different kind of fact from the one concerning the kinds of the relations that we do imagine. I am accustomed to calling these other kinds of facts *artifacts,* thereby emphasizing their reliance on appearance, material conditions, and artistic making. Here I simply want to insist that we need to think about the pragmatics of imagining relations rather than allowing ourselves be defeated from the outset by doubts about the facticity of relation itself.

A pragmatic emphasis requires that we characterize the particular

---

description of willing as a function that single-handedly creates an individual's destiny, despite the most adverse circumstances. Cornelius Castoriadis, incidentally, makes the valuable point that Arendt's followers mistakenly believe, under the force of her reading, that Kant resolved the conflict between autonomy and heteronomy (1991, 88).

4. The exposure of this "error" is a constant theme in both Continental and American deconstruction. Derrida (1978, 169–74), for instance, deconstructs the logic of relation via an analysis of exemplarity, while Paul de Man (1979, 151–52) debunks relation as a failed metaphor.

The Subject and Other Subjects

ways that religion, aesthetics, ethics, and politics imagine what a good relation is. In what form does relation appear to us in each mode? If it is the case, as I insist, that having successful experiences of relation relies on our ability to find ways of imagining different forms of goodness, this question is hardly trivial. It is in fact the most difficult and urgent question that we might pose.

In religion, the sublime appears as the felt experience of a higher and unknowable power of understanding by whom or by which our lack of understanding is repaired. The experience of the sublime focuses on an object that appears as more than it is, thereby defeating our ability to understand it and summoning thoughts of someone for whom the object is not a mystery. God symbolizes this superior understanding, an understanding for which we have no conception other than the sacred itself. That is, we know God, without really knowing him, via a deficiency in our own thinking. The sacred represents collective agreement in the form of a leap of faith in the existence of a mind or state of being capable of harmonizing the diverse experiences of human beings with each other and with the object world. Agreement and commensurability are God as such.

In the case of aesthetics, beauty emerges as an aura of agreement felt by everyone confronted by an object. This object requires us to name it as beautiful, without, however, our being able to say what beauty is. Beauty *is* because people agree that it exists, without setting out to reach an agreement about it beforehand.

The imagination of ethical goodness would appear to be more arduous, but only if we underestimate how very difficult is the concept of beauty. The ethical good aims at the representation of a person in whom we imagine character. Character, like beauty, is a form of consensus, but we locate this consensus not in the people joining in the presence of the object but within the person who is said to possess virtue, which is to say that we perceive the person of character as possessing inner harmony and strength of will. Character, unlike beauty, is not without concepts. We can—and often do—write a recipe for it. And yet, possessing the recipe does not ensure that we will attain virtue, so that the end effect of experiencing ethical goodness embodied in a character is not unlike the mysterious sensation of standing before a beautiful painting. It is no accident that a historical confusion exists between beauty and goodness, because we view character as beautiful and, consequently, are led to hope that beauty also possesses ethical goodness. So "Beauty is truth, truth beauty," as Keats put it. Kant has the best language to explain this confusion. He explains that ethics requires an aesthetics of morals to make it accessible to human understanding. The aesthetic component of ethics lies precisely in the huge chasm between our understanding of what character is and our ability to perform the prescribed actions that will build or exercise it. The crossing of this chasm seems a mysterious leap of faith, beyond prescription, the result being that the virtuous person is as beautiful as he or she is good.

If we define politics in terms of alliances between communities, its goodness is perhaps the most obvious of all. Consensus between political bodies is peace. When I say that peace is the most obvious form of the political good, however, I do not mean to undercut its difficulty. While the experience of beauty is compelled yet unfathomable and the experience of character is fathomable yet unachievable, the experience of peace is impossible to locate in any one person, object, or symbol. Peace presents a serious problem of representation. It is not a god. It is not a work of art. It is not a saint or a portrait of the good will. It cannot be symbolized by a building or public space, although it is important to understand the role of monuments, courthouses, and other architectural wonders in our imagination of the concept of the state or of justice. Peace appears to be the opposite of the work of art, which is an object lacking a concept. Peace is a concept without one object, which is another way of saying that it is a concept with many objects. And this is a way of saying that we rely on other modes of relation to imagine the political good, these other modes most obviously being aesthetics, ethics, and religion.

Each mode provides a particular resource used to compensate for our lack of political imagination. The aesthetic mode lends itself to the creation of political artifacts, although their ability to signify the political good remains inadequate. Symbolic objects such as flags may represent harmonious political bodies, but we experience these objects not with distinctive political emotions but as aesthetic objects, as beautiful. Different nations appreciate and protect traveling exhibits of artifacts, but the ultimate meaning of the exhibits remains lodged in the objects themselves, there being no supplementary symbolism there to represent the good political relations that made the traveling exhibit possible. (Peace is, however, a bit like a museum in that people go to museums to look at objects but often end up contemplating each other; the artifacts in museums become an occasion for an experience of social harmony but only if they are somehow ignored.)

Ethics helps to embody our desire for political direction and relation in individual human beings. Political leaders hold out to citizens the hope of peace, the idea of a strong nation, or of a manifest political destiny, but we experience these leaders in ethical terms as courageous, honorable, and loving (or in aesthetic terms as charismatic, graceful, and handsome). Historically, of course, great houses have been wed to join political bodies, while today our leaders shake hands, embrace, kiss, and exchange smiles to much fanfare. We read these gestures as political alliance. But what we are really seeing are traditional representations of the successful joinings between individuals, which explains why political commentators and politicians alike are so quick to talk about the friendships that arise between heads of state during political negotiations. Ethics comes to the rescue to repair the gap in our imagination of politics. For friendship is, finally, an ethical representation, albeit strongly integrated into the tradition of political science.

Once upon a time, of course, we imagined nations in terms of their religious worship. The god of the clan, Robertson Smith declared, is the clan itself, and Durkheim used the idea of "collective representation" to capture the same mode of religious imagination.[5] Religious representation was for centuries the privileged vehicle by which communities imagined themselves, but once God died and secularization was set into motion as a historical force, it became increasingly difficult for human beings to place their faith in such representations. The opening up of the world has also made it more difficult for communities to represent their uniqueness in terms of their objects of worship since increasingly communities share religious objects. The vestiges of the old alliance between religious and political representation remain everywhere we look, but they no longer possess for the most part the power necessary to imagine the state of being of good, collective human relating. We easily ally ourselves with the totemic symbols of groups, such as the mascots of sport teams, but no one really believes any more that the lion, for example, is an adequate symbol for the unique properties and cohesiveness of the football team playing in Detroit.

Politics appears to rely on no special form of representation. It might be objected that there is a reason for this, and a very commonsensical one at that. Political harmony must be negotiated. But it is not particularly easy to imagine the form that these negotiations would take. In the modern world, in fact, it is as if the very idea of negotiation compensates for our inability to imagine peace. Trade now provides the preferred language of international relations. The leveling

---

5. See William Robertson Smith (1894) and Emile Durkheim (1968) for the earliest attempts to define religion and social structure as mirror images of one another.

effect of the market, some people believe, will adjust the differences between nations, put them on an equal footing, and harmonize potential conflicts. "Peace through business" might be the slogan of modern international relations. And yet, while everyone wants to make a profit, the profit motive has never been a firm guarantee against exploitation, and it does not take a long glance at the globe to realize that the international market divides different nations into enclaves defined by their raw materials, cheap labor, and advanced technology. International business is more interested in maintaining the distinctive character of these enclaves in order to exploit their role in a larger chain of production than it is in leveling the playing field and producing long-term, beneficial relations between nations.

Politics and Eternal Rest

Given the failure of human beings to imagine the relation of goodness in politics, it is not surprising that they would choose to represent this failure itself as the political good. And so Kant's philosopher dreams his sweet dream of peace, alternately imagining the perpetual harmony of the starry heavens above and the eternal rest of the graveyard below. In both cases, the symbol of perpetual peace is death. Perhaps this explains why Kant opens his essay by making a double bargain with death. First, he presents the desire for perpetual peace as a joke, engaging in a bit of gallows's humor at the expense of humanity. The Dutch shopkeeper's sign makes a mockery of the common fate of philosophers, politicians, and citizens, throwing together peacemakers and warmongers, all of whom court death to make their dreams of perpetual peace come true. Second, Kant signs a peace treaty with the powers of the state, with those who cannot get enough of war and death, hoping to disclaim in advance any disloyal opinions that they might assign to him. But you do not sign a peace treaty unless you are or expect to be at war. Kant has one foot in the grave not only because he desires perpetual peace but because he dares to give advice about the political life of his community, for he lives in a country ruled by men who do not always take kindly to such advice.

Kant's essay, then, amounts to a confession that the state holds the power of death over him. "The practical politician," he knows, "tends to look down with great smugness on the political theorist, regarding him as an academic whose empty ideas cannot endanger the nation" (1983, 107). Consequently, Kant reasons, "the theorist is allowed to fire his entire volley, without the *worldly-wise* statesman becoming the least bit concerned" (107). And yet Kant also knows that his life will be at risk if that same statesman "detects some danger to the nation" in his views (107). Kant signs a peace treaty with the state only to get the chance to fire his entire volley, hoping that those who hold the power of death over him will not notice his declaration of war. We should notice, however, that his peace treaty fails to meet his first article for the establishment of perpetual peace: "No treaty of peace that tacitly reserves issues for a future war shall be held valid" (107). Kant's intention is to wage a future war for peace, and so his essay begins by establishing the conditions of free speech by which he hopes to wage that war.

While Kant surely has the right to speak freely about his hopes for the future of his country without being harmed by the political powers that be, he cannot hold the same expectation with regard to his fellow citizens. Participation in politics is bought at a price, and that price, Kant understands, is the potential sacrifice of individual persons. His thoughts here are probably focused on the most immediate threat to his liberty, the monarchy of King Frederick William II, but his theory of democracy, to which I will soon turn, also reveals that political form is inherently sacrificial—that the political life of the state is somehow married to the sacrifice of citizens. The desire for perpetual peace—the relation of the good in politics—always collaborates with eternal rest—with the death wish in human relationships, and that death wish is experienced most vividly by the individual members of a community, since they are the locus of its emotions.

Kant obviously fears that Frederick William II will reprimand him. It is perhaps less obvious that he fears his fellow citizens. Nevertheless, Kant shows an increasing preoccupation with this last concern as his essay progresses toward its conclusion, demonstrating ultimately more terror of violence within nations than of violence between them. The first half of the essay has a political emphasis, presenting five preliminary articles for establishing perpetual peace between nations, while the second half focuses on ethical matters, arguing about which forms of government best eliminate conflicts between individuals. Surprisingly, only two of the five articles in the early part of the essay involve efforts to disarm war powers.[6] Kant is concerned first and fore-

---

6. Kant's five articles are worth reviewing briefly if only to remind us of his diplomatic prowess and continuing relevance to peace studies:
    1. No treaty of peace that tacitly reserves issues for future war shall be held valid.
    2. No independent nation, be it large or small, may be acquired by another nation by inheritance, exchange, purchase, or gift.

most with establishing the right of separate nations to exist autonomously and only afterward with protecting these nations against conquest by other countries. For example, he maintains that countries have the obligation to preserve their own national interests before they come to the aid of other countries. The point to stress here is that these articles are purely political, for they do not flirt with the utopian desire to banish separate nations in the favor of a single world government. If world peace is ever to exist, it will be created through the good offices of many separate and different countries working together as a league of nations.

The last half of the essay, however, focuses actively on the internal affairs of nations. Kant's first definitive article of perpetual peace, for example, requires that "the civil constitution of every nation should be republican" (1983, 112). At first glance, this article seems to conceal an attack against the monarchy of Frederick William II. In fact, Kant makes the case that the monarchy should be supported because it will gradually evolve into a republican government, while protecting its citizens in the meantime against the most dangerous form of government—democracy: "*democracy*, in the proper sense of the term," Kant laments, "is necessarily a *despotism*, because it sets up an executive power in which all citizens make decisions about and, if need be against one (who therefore does not agree); consequently, all, who are not quite all, decide, so that the general will contradicts both itself and freedom" (114). In short, Kant pledges allegiance to the king and to republicanism to contain the spread of democracy, and what he fears most about democracy is the potential violence and lack of feeling of its citizenry.

Kant wants to tame the violence of democracy—what he calls the despotism of the all turning against the one—and he believes that republicanism will accomplish the feat because it establishes a separation of powers and delegates authorities to shield individual citizens from the violence of others. In reality, however, republican government only softens but does not eliminate the sacrifices required by politics. Usually Kant represents these sacrifices in terms of a gap between ethical and political conduct. He explains, for example, that no single person has the ability to transform the particular desires of

---

3. Standing armies *(miles perpetuus)* shall be gradually abolished.

4. No national debt shall be contracted in connection with the foreign affairs of the nation.

5. No nation shall forcibly interfere with the constitution and government of another.

(1983, 107–11)

citizens into a common will, and yet he insists that the moral politician will see it as a duty to fight for laws that uphold the commonweal, stressing that "this ought to be done even at the cost of self-sacrifice" (1983, 128). Ethics and politics do not always serve the same ends, and when their ends differ, moral politicians suffer, for duty compels them to speak out on behalf of the community as a whole, but there is no way for them to know whether this same community will not turn against them with great violence.

The political relation, I have argued, is beyond the ken of any given individual. It arises whenever two or more groups begin a negotiation, whether peaceful or violent. A more sophisticated definition—one not without value for conceptualizing the gap between ethical and political representation—would define the political as the negotiation between two or more groups defined not as collections of individuals but as sets of rules. In effect, conceiving of society as a set of rules gives it the status of the mathematical sublime for each individual in that society. While I might understand, for example, that my community consists of a defining set of rules, complete with an origin and history of change and interpretation, these rules are ultimately as incomprehensible to me as an infinite number string, like π, so I have no choice but to accept them though a leap of faith amounting to the simple conviction that my community does exist as an entity and that I am part of it, even though I cannot begin to imagine what it is or how I might fit into it. Living in common exposes individuals to a constant state of bewilderment about who they should try to be or about what they should try to do. But this is only the beginning of the dilemma of political life. For two sets of rules cannot have an encounter without the mediation of an interpreting agent. That is, one individual or more is always necessary to interpret the rules, intentions, and interests of the group, so that political encounters necessarily degenerate (and I use the word undisparagingly) into ethical encounters between individuals who must think and act with conviction, even though they are not sure what they are doing.

Here is where the sacrificial structure of politics becomes most apparent. For one interpretation is always subject to another one, and if any given interpretation is rejected or leads to disaster, the interpreter will carry the blame for it. History abounds with the stories of individuals, great-hearted and mean-spirited alike, who have borne the burden of "bad" interpretations, who have dared to define in the unique timbre of one voice the many voices of their society. Politics is a space of tragedy, I have already mentioned, but of a tragedy of the individual, because it requires the passionate but disinterested pursuit of ends that do not profit individuals in the short term, and yet it asks these passionate individuals to put aside their enthusiasm for the common purpose at a moment's notice to preserve the common purpose. Social existence places constraints on individuals with the promise of celebrating their virtue should they accept these constraints, but it often sacrifices them in the process, tearing their life from them at the very moment when they are trying hardest to be good.

The moral incoherence of politics is, for Kant, an effect of group behavior—of the dissymmetry implicit in relations of self and other. Individuals, for example, believe that they are themselves honest but fail to believe in the honesty of other people. Nevertheless, morality does give proof of its universal claim on the human imagination in the individual's wish that everyone abide by a sense of right conduct, even as this same individual doubts that his or her right conduct will be reciprocated and turns to evil as a result. Kant's entire project is designed to cut the Gordian knot of such dilemmas by separating the specific content of moral behavior from its formal conditions and then giving preference to form. Consequently, Kant adduces a principle of right behavior that no longer focuses on a specific material end: for example, the desire to arrange your behavior so that you are not cheated by others because you are more honest than they. This new moral imperative substitutes a formal end for a specific material end, requiring that this end apply categorically: "Act so that you will that your maxim ought to become a universal law (no matter what the end may be)" (1983, 132). In the final analysis, the categorical imperative is merely a conceptual tool used to measure the formal conditions of an end against its material and social ones; it frees individuals from the influence of other people and puts them in touch with the autonomy of their own moral judgment, in effect enclosing each person in a space of moral secrecy where the freedom to be good can be experienced in private.

Formally, then, the conflict between ethics and politics disappears, or we might say that individuals make it disappear by imagining that they live only with themselves and not with other people. One might conclude with only the slightest irony that only the last man alive on earth is free, finally, to express his true moral nature, since he would no longer be paralyzed by mistrust of other people's honesty. The categorical imperative imagines every person on earth as the last survivor. But the world has not yet come to this, and human beings must live common lives, and so the conflict between ethics and politics reappears whenever we return to the sphere of practice. Here the fate of moral individuals turns tragic once more, since they must accept the sacrifices required to defend right conduct, and Kant cannot simply dispense with their sacrifices but must honor them. Moral individuals show true courage, Kant proclaims, by not yielding to evil but by pressing on more boldly than their fate allows. They sacrifice themselves for the common good and are lamented, unlike many others whose deaths are sordid and violent and right only insofar they demonstrate the power of morality negatively. These last lawless creatures seek to violate others who are just as lawlessly disposed toward them, and thus all become caught in a storm of violence and greed, destroying themselves as if by their own hand.

Kant, it appears, cannot speak about politics without returning to ethics. It could be argued that this is a weakness in his philosophical system. I prefer to argue, however, that he runs up against the limits of the political imagination and presses on against this obstacle more boldly than the moral imagination allows. The result is reasoning to the brink of unreason, philosophical failure, but not a failure of nerve. For Kant dares to push his thought into areas where it is doomed to fail.

Perpetual Peace concludes with such a failure. This failure bears no resemblance to the note of ultimate failure with which Kant begins his essay when he jokes that only death will provide the solution to incessant warfare. Rather, it is a philosophical failure of great richness, for Kant topples his entire moral edifice in the hope of discovering one principle that will allow him both to imagine political harmony and to bring to an end the warfare between ethics and politics. The principle is *publicity*. In ethics, we recall, individuals who are considering an action converse with themselves, seeking to apply the categorical imperative to their action. The conversation of these persons is wholly internal, secreted in the being of the person, constitutive of that being in its special relation to moral reasoning, since a "person" is for Kant only that place where reason makes its appearance—and where reason appears, of course, freedom also appears. In the case of political right, however, the conversation takes place between individuals or nations in public. Kant claims that publicity is "found *a priori* in reason" (1983, 135) and insists that it may be used in the place of the categorical imperative as the test of moral politics. He even provides a transcendental formula of political right based on the categorical form: "All actions that affect the rights of other men are wrong if their maxim is not consistent with publicity" (135). Thus, if the plans of a state cannot be made public, without destroying its hopes for enacting them, Kant reasons, they should be ruled immoral. If a people cannot overthrow an oppressive tyrant without the use of secrecy, the revolt is wrong (but so will be the attempt of the tyrant to regain power, if he uses secrecy to do it). In short, Kant replaces in one fell swoop the logic of moral reasoning with the principle of publicity, as if morality and consensus were one and the same. Kant's private moral self becomes mass man.

After years of describing the individual as an end in itself, Kant shifts in *Perpetual Peace* to a concept in which the autonomy of individual self-reflection is placed at risk. The individual is no longer permitted to choose a course of action without first seeking the agreement of the community at large. At the moment when Kant wants most to avoid violence to the individual, then, he embraces the solution most antagonistic to what an individual is: he saves the individual from harm by literally erasing the concept of autonomy itself—the very concept on which his claim to philosophical prominence rests.[7] Perhaps, this misguided maneuver tells us more about what an individual is than we want to know. It suggests that human beings are never more individual than when they are subject to violence, subjugation, and nonexistence, and that we cannot save individuals by sparing them this fate, though try we must, since it ends by robbing them of individuality itself. It is because the moral imagination overrides the political imagination and finds its truest expression in the individual that individual human beings suffer political violence. The sad truth is that ethics rarely combines successfully with politics. Aesthetics more easily combines with politics, although the payment for the combination may also be high in victims.

The relation between self and other in the political context, whether we are considering one community or more, presents no analogy by which we might imagine it. Its harmony, rules of coherence, its existence as a conceptual fact—if there are such things as harmony, coherence, and facts among human beings who breathe—possess no symbols or objects by which we might bring them to life in our mind. Thoughts of sublime gods, virtuous heroes, or beautiful paintings may give us repose on a day-to-day basis, but they offer no solutions to the misunderstandings of existence in common. Nor does the political imagination appear to have anything to do with the model of the part

---

7. A final attempt to formulate a transcendental principle of political right shows how far Kant goes to merge ethics and politics. He seems to forget the idea, central to the categorical imperative, that individuals achieve autonomy by giving the law to themselves, choosing instead to make publicity—in effect, heteronomy—the key to ending lawlessness: "All maxims that *require* publicity (in order not to fail of their end) agree with both politics and morality" (1983, 139).

and the whole.⁸ Individuals compose society, but they are only social members by virtue of the existence and history of that society. And yet this society is realized in the individuals created by it. It is only in them that society exists at all. There is no analogy for this type of relationship elsewhere. It has to be thought and known as itself.

Perhaps this is why we imagine the good political relation by way of our own death. The graveyard is the one place where there is no difference between one individual and many others—the one place where ethics and politics join in perpetual peace. It is as if there were no way to symbolize a peaceful community except by returning to the sacrificial scene located at the origin of symbolicity itself, where every word arises as a capstone and a memorial, a place of death and a plot against future deaths.⁹

The plight of free people is everywhere the same. We value the freedom of the individual person above everything else, but it is this person of great value whom we must sacrifice in particular cases, standing by as individual citizens lose their liberty and life, so that the freedom of everyone else will survive—as if the freedom and harmony of all were directly connected to the willingness of the one to die for the all. Perhaps they are. This is the most shocking truth about our existence—what allies it to death and what tempts every peace-loving person in every free nation to dream Kant's sweet dream.

The citizen of the free nation has—and always will have—one foot in the grave.

---

8. My discussion here paraphrases Castoriadis's remarks (1991, 145).

9. Or, to put it another way, the failure of linguistic representation, so celebrated in current debates, is everywhere and always a failure of political representation, although the conjoining of these two types of representation alters the conception of the political, since it is established on what must be called a prepolitical scene. I allude, of course, to René Girard's claim that victimage is the origin of symbolicity (1978, 177). The work of Eric Gans also focuses on the relation of violence to the origin of language. Among his many books the most concise is perhaps *Originary Thinking: Elements of Generative Anthropology* (1993).

Conclusion

In some high schools in the American South, two prom queens are chosen each fall, one black, one white. A young woman's name has been submitted in nomination. Her mother is white, and her father is black. The school officials require that she declare herself as one color or the other if her name is to be placed on the ballot. She refuses and withdraws from the competition in protest. A young Native American woman remarks to a roving reporter that she does not fit into either category.

It is time for the annual Miss America beauty contest. As in previous years, voices are raised against the bathing-suit competition because it objectifies women. Other voices express concern that some contestants have had their figures enhanced by plastic surgery.

Along the Mexican border in California security is tight. It has become a question whether illegal aliens should be eligible for government health care in the United States. Enforcement is a problem. Mexican Americans look just like Mexicans. Some have proposed issuing a national identity card. Others argue that a national identity card would infringe upon the rights and freedom of American citizens.

These three controversies tell us something about the complex relationship between ethical, aesthetic, and political subjectivity. First, if character or personal identity were easily recognized, not as an end in itself, but as an objective quality, we would not be troubled by the request of school officials that a young woman in a popularity contest decide whether her "self" is going to be read as black or white. Ethical sensitivity requires, however, that persons be granted the freedom to determine their own ends, even though freedom is hardly anyone's to possess. Second, if aesthetics were our primary concern, we would raise no objection to determining the worth of a person on the basis of appearance and body shape. The aesthetic attitude measures the qualities of objects, bodies are objects with specific qualities, and yet we also understand that people are objectified by aesthetic preoccupations, and we rightly find this objectification morally repugnant. Finally, if politics ruled our conception of geography, and not ethics, we would not care whether noncitizens received medical care. Politics justly lays down the limits of inclusion for communities, whether it involves groups internal to its borders or whether it is policing external borders. There can be no political community without a serious conception of borders. It is unreasonable to expect anything else of the political mode. Nevertheless, we are disturbed by politics, and we are most disturbed when politics is most itself, when it is most successful in limiting the inclusiveness of our communities. Borders look arbitrary because we are compelled by the moral judgment that lines drawn between people always raise the specter of violence between them. "Good fences make good neighbors" is a political truism that ethical thought necessarily abhors.

More important, these three controversies reveal that ethics always has the last word, even the last word about itself. Ethics stands as the ultimate judge in matters of the subject, making sure that the individual person be conceived always as a subject and never as a mere object. This means that the very idea of a "subject," despite recent attempts to conceive of it as a reification or objectification, is first and foremost the site of an ethical resistance against the tendency to think of selves as things, its most revolutionary expression being found in Kant, who defines personhood not as a means to an end but as an end in itself, that is, as the appearance of a radical finitude unintelligible in terms of any other object or subject whatsoever. In Kantian terms, the subject is where freedom makes its most radical appearance, insofar as freedom can be said to be anywhere.

It does not require much reflection to understand that ethics makes it difficult to conceive of the notion of the subject as such. The world of identity is a world of differences, and ethics refuses to live in a world of real differences, since its conception of reality rebels against the creation of any object that might stand apart from the equalizing effect of the eternal return of the same. Husserl was surely right that consciousness is always consciousness of something, but it is also true that when the identity of the subject is limited to its objects of consciousness, the subject is more often than not reduced to a mere thing. The self becomes conscious of itself through the mediation of its objects of consciousness, including other subjects, but these objects risk to reify the nature of any given subject, because determinations about subjects are hardly possible without reducing them to their objects.

Ethics refuses in its purest form to place limits on subjectivity. It

Conclusion

therefore perceives the mediation of objects as a real and valid threat to selfhood, for mediation usually implies objectification. In fact, to speculate that ethics has a proper object, an object of its own, is to conclude that ethics has failed. The radically interpersonal context required by ethics represents a sphere in which the creation of any object is in some way the objectification of a person. Ethics insists on conceiving subjectivity in its most radical expression, therefore, precisely in order to rob itself of a proper object. We are dealing here in philosophical abstractions, of course, but the crucial and common conflicts about identity that arise everyday expose that these philosophical abstractions are not any less pertinent for being so abstract. Debates about essentialism in philosophical quarters, for example, seem unworldly and irrelevant to our daily lives, and yet they parallel debates about the problems of sexual objectification or racial stereotyping found everywhere in our society, and these problems cut to the core of our existence. Each is about the limits placed on some subjects by other subjects. Each shows some subjects treating other subjects like objects. Our disdain for such practices is not merely a matter of political correctness or philosophical daintiness. Objectification is a form of cruelty. It is not for nothing, then, that it has such bad press. Its history is long and sordid. In a certain sense, we can conceive of nothing as hostile to subjects as the tendency to objectify them.

In another sense, however, objectification seems to be the primary condition of subjectivity, and if we conceive of it as repressive, we must conclude that repression is a condition of subjectivity as well. The sad truth is that we would have no identity at all, private or public, if repression did not in some way hold sway over us. This is the case whether we are discussing psychological ideas of repression or political ones. Psychological speaking, it is clear that one identity emerges and achieves coherence only by excluding other identities. Investment in one object necessarily means noninvestment in another. Repression is the mechanism, according to classic psychoanalytic theory, by which we internalize the objects that make up our personalities. It stings us with feelings of anxiety because the internalization of an object always translates as the loss of a person important to us, and with the loss of this person comes a certain loss of perception. "Thus, the first determinant of anxiety, which the ego itself introduces," Freud explains, "is loss of perception of the object (which is equated with the loss of the object itself)" (1966–74, 20:170). The internalization of the object appears designed to halt the pain of mourning, but in fact the process only repeats the trauma because an object internalized remains a source of anxiety. The loss of other subjects from the field of perception is the primary wound that repression seeks to heal. From this healing arises something like a history of identifications and an accompanying subjectivity, and yet the subject never frees itself from anxiety for the simple reason that it must repeat the pattern of loss and internalization at every instant of its waking and dreaming existence.

Repression is painful, but its anxieties are in fact the birth pangs of subjectivity. An identity is a history of lost attachments—attachments whose subjective qualities have been sacrificed in the process of internalizing them. These lost subjects are remembered as internal objects, each one coming to signify a particular feature or trait in our personality. They mediate between the world and us, helping and harming us long after we have ceased to mourn their loss. Christopher Bollas, for example, argues that "the constant objectification of the self for purposes of thinking is commonplace" (1987, 42). Thought cannot occur without objectification: every individual "may objectify, imagine, analyse and manage the self through identification with primary others" (41). All of us have adopted certain gaits or position ourselves in space and time because of the way that our caretakers walked or held our bodies. These traits are viewed as properties of personal style, but they are also products of objectification. Neither extreme exists without the other. A self is always another's object, and most of us manage the care of ourselves as if our self were our most precious object.

Human beings become human subjects by relating to themselves and others as objects, even though we seem most human when we aspire not to do so. Political repression presents an excessive version of this process. It takes the natural tensions and conflicts of intersubjective relations and attempts to make of them a system of coercion. It would make of all citizens the type of subject required by those in power to maintain their power. I do not think, however, that political repression is a necessary component of human subjectivity. A great deal of modern thought seems to have lost track of the very real differences between systematic political repression and the supposedly repressive nature of communal life as such. Totalitarianism and dictatorship are not merely the natural fulfillment of the coercive trends of communal existence. The lines of descent of terror do not move with ease down a slippery slope connecting the demands made on individuals by living among others of their kind to the cruel restrictions legislated by unjust political regimes. Society is not an unnatural prison but the natural habitat of human beings, and political repression has no place in it.

Conclusion

Nevertheless, life in common, especially political life, does expose individuals to disapproval and sanctions, and these checks on enthusiasm and thought are bound to be experienced as repressive. The political sphere is one in which individuals speak about the future of their life in common, and disagreements are bound to happen and equally bound to have violent consequences. The damage will be more psychological than physical, if the society is relatively healthy, but this fact is of little consolation to the injured party whose pain is part of the creation and maintenance of the public sphere. Politics is always sacrificial, for we need to witness the sacrifices of individuals to maintain a sense of political cohesion. It is hardly something to celebrate, but it seems an unavoidable fact of social existence. Rousseau, of course, defined *obligation* as the irritating responsibility of being in another person's presence. He experienced it as if it were a unique call upon him alone, despised it, tried to flee from it, and failed. All modern subjects have followed in his footsteps in one way or another. But Rousseau refused to see that obligation is a two-way street. It resembles a social glue. We feel the compulsion to serve others just as readily as we feel the need to call others to our service. Rousseau also refused to see that he could not free himself from suffering by fleeing from his obligations, for freedom is more painful than obligation in the final analysis. Freedom is experienced in society as breaking the bonds of society itself. Human beings cannot free themselves from social obligations without cutting themselves off from other human beings, but when they do, they invariably bring suffering upon themselves and others, since we are meant to live together. Attempts have been made—and will be made again—to place curbs on freedom in order to prevent the suffering that it causes. We accept the fact, by and large, that we have the right to our freedom as long as we do not harm other people. But there is no individual freedom without harming others. And there is no way to prevent freedom from bringing about harm to one person without causing harm to another person. This is why I have called political existence a space of tragedy, but a tragedy of the individual. Sacrifice and sorrow define the conditions of existence of the individual living among others of his or her kind. We become subjects, and subjects gather into communities, by being subjected to the redundant logic of human sacrifice.

Our ethical distaste with the redundancy of violence and with the forms of repression enacted in its name is at once the sublime achievement of modern morality and its imbecilic undoing. In the name of ethics we disdain the injustices of this world, and we are right to do it. Ethical thought bestows remarkable critical power upon us. And yet our nausea with the world also transports ethics beyond the sphere of human action and appearance, embracing a nether world of dizzying forms and formalities designed to avoid what is most human about us. No human body—and all human beings have bodies—can measure up to the ethical idea of how human bodies should inhabit the earth. Human beings, because they are things of this world, make their presence known and perform actions among other actions, creating an existence for themselves, making shining and shabby artifacts, and effecting sudden shifts in their sphere of influence, all of which are bound to act violently and adversely on what is already there. Ethics is sublime in its hatred of cruelty, injustice, and sacrifice; it is idiotic in its forgetfulness that bodies cannot inhabit the earth without sanctioning cruelty, injustice, and sacrifice.

We are of this earth—that is perhaps the source of our greatest nobility as a species. We feel compelled to change the earth under our very feet, depriving ourselves of the only home we will ever have—this is perhaps the source of our greatest tragedy. The irony is that nobility and tragedy can be reversed with a simple somersault of human thought, as we reconceive our debt to the earth as our tragedy and our desire to change it as our noblest aim. One truth is no less compelling than the other, and human truth has not suffered any less because of it. Nor have we.

References

Anzaldúa, Gloria. 1988. "Tlilla, Tla palli: The Path of the Red and Black Ink." In *Multi-Cultural Literacy*, ed. Rick Simonson and Scott Walker, 29–40. Saint Paul, Minn.: Greywolf Press.
Arendt, Hannah. 1955. *Men in Dark Times*. New York: Harcourt, Brace and World.
———. 1958. *The Human Condition*. Chicago: University of Chicago Press.
———. 1968. *Between Past and Future*. New York: Viking Press.
———. 1977. "Public Rights and Private Interests: In Response to Charles Frankel." In *Small Comforts for Hard Times*, ed. M. Mooney and F. Stubner, 103–8. New York: Columbia University Press.
———. 1982. *Lectures on Kant's Political Philosophy*. Ed. Ronald Beiner. Chicago: University of Chicago Press.
Aristotle. 1983. *The Nicomachean Ethics*. Trans. David Ross. 1925. Reprint, New York: Oxford University Press.
Asante, Molefi Kete. 1992. "Multiculturalism: An Exchange." In *Debating P.C.: The Controversy Over Political Correctness on College Campuses*, ed. Paul Berman, 299–311. New York: Laurel.
Baldwin, James. 1988. "A Talk to Teachers." In *Multi-Cultural Literacy*, ed. Rick Simonson and Scott Walker, 3–12. Saint Paul, Minn.: Greywolf Press.
Barthes, Roland. 1977. "Introduction to the Structural Analysis of Narratives." In *Image, Music, Text*, trans. Stephen Heath, 79–124. New York: Farrar, Straus and Giroux.
Benhabib, Seyla. 1992. *Situating the Self: Gender, Community, and Postmodernism in Contemporary Ethics*. New York: Routledge.
Benjamin, Walter. 1968. "The Storyteller." In *Illuminations: Essays and Reflections*, ed. Hannah Arendt, trans. Harry Zohn. New York: Schocken.
———. 1977. *The Origin of German Tragic Drama*. Trans. John Osborne. London: NLB.
Bloom, Allan. 1987. *The Closing of the American Mind*. New York: Simon and Schuster.

References

Bollas, Christopher. 1987. *The Shadow of the Object: Psychoanalysis of the Unthought Unknown.* New York: Columbia University Press.
Booth, Wayne C. 1988. *The Company We Keep: An Ethics of Fiction.* Berkeley and Los Angeles: University of California Press.
Butler, Judith. 1990. *Gender Trouble: Feminism and the Subversion of Identity.* New York: Routledge.
———. 1992. "Contingent Foundations: Feminism and the Question of 'Postmodernism.'" In *Feminists Theorize the Political,* ed. Judith Butler and Joan W. Scott, 3–21. New York: Routledge.
Canovan, Margaret. 1985. "Politics as Culture: Hannah Arendt and the Public Realm." *History of Political Thought* 6 (winter): 617–42.
Castoriadis, Cornelius. 1991. *Philosophy, Politics, Autonomy.* Ed. David Ames Curtis. New York: Oxford University Press.
Cavell, Stanley. 1969. "Music Decomposed." In *Must We Mean What We Say? A Book of Essays.* New York: Scribner.
———. 1994. *A Pitch of Philosophy: Autobiographical Exercises.* Cambridge, Mass.: Harvard University Press.
Danto, Arthur. 1964. "The Artworld." *Journal of Philosophy* 61:571–84.
———. 1992. *Beyond the Brillo Box: The Visual Arts in the Post-Historical Perspective.* New York: Farrar, Straus and Giroux.
De Man, Paul. 1979. *Allegories of Reading.* New Haven, Conn.: Yale University Press.
———. 1984. *The Rhetoric of Romanticism.* New York: Columbia University Press.
D'Entrèves, Maurizio Passerin. 1992. "Hannah Arendt and the Idea of Citizenship." In *Dimensions of Radical Democracy,* ed. Chantal Mouffe, 145–68. New York: Verso.
Derrida, Jacques. 1978. "La Parole soufflée." In *Writing and Difference,* trans. Alan Bass, 169–95. Chicago: University of Chicago Press.
———. 1979. *Spurs: Nietzsche's Styles.* Trans. Barbara Harlow. Chicago: University of Chicago Press.
———. 1980. *La Carte postale: De Socrate à Freud et au-delà.* Paris: Flammarion.
———. 1988. *Limited Inc.* Trans. Samuel Weber and Jeffrey Mehlman. Evanston, Ill.: Northwestern University Press.
D'Souza, Dinesh. 1991. *Illiberal Education: The Politics of Race and Sex on Campus.* New York: Free Press.
———. 1992. "The Big Chill? Interview with Dinesh D'Souza." Interview by Robert MacNeil. In *Debating P.C.: The Controversy over Political Correctness on College Campuses,* ed. Paul Berman, 29–39. New York: Laurel.
Durkheim, Émile. 1968. *Les Formes élémentaires de la vie religieuse.* Paris: PUF.
Durand, Steven. 1989. "Censorship, Multiculturalism, and Symbols." *High Performance* 12 (fall): 40–41.

Eagleton, Terry. 1990. *The Ideology of the Aesthetic.* London: Blackwell.
Ferry, Luc. 1993. *Homo Aestheticus: The Invention of Taste in the Democratic Age.* Trans. Robert de Loaiza. Chicago: University of Chicago Press.
Foucault, Michel. 1970. *The Order of Things: An Archaeology of the Human Sciences.* New York: Random House.
———. 1980. *The History of Sexuality.* Volume 1: *An Introduction.* Trans. Robert Hurley. New York: Vintage Books.
———. 1985. *The History of Sexuality.* Volume 2: *The Uses of Pleasure.* Trans. Robert Hurley. New York: Pantheon.
Freud, Sigmund. 1966–74. *The Standard Edition of the Complete Psychological Works of Sigmund Freud.* 24 volumes. Ed. and trans. James Strachey. London: Hogarth Press.
Gadamer, Hans-Georg. 1975. "The Subjectivisation of Aesthetics in the Kantian Critique" In *Truth and Method.* New York: Seabury Press.
Gans, Eric. 1993. *Originary Thinking: Elements of Generative Anthropology.* Stanford, Calif.: Stanford University Press.
Geertz, Clifford. 1973. *The Interpretation of Cultures.* New York: Basic Books.
———. 1984. "Distinguished Lecture: Anti Anti-Relativism." *American Anthropologist* 86:263–78.
———. 1985a. "Waddling In." *Times Literary Supplement,* 7 June, 623–24.
———. 1985b. *Works and Lives: The Anthropologist as Author.* Stanford, Calif.: Stanford University Press.
———. 1986. "The Uses of Diversity." *Michigan Quarterly Review* 25:105–23.
Gilligan, Carol. 1982. *In a Different Voice: Psychological Theory and Women's Development.* Cambridge, Mass.: Harvard University Press.
Girard, René. 1978. "Differentiation and Reciprocity in Lévi-Strauss and Contemporary Theory." In *"To Double Business Bound": Essays on Literature, Mimesis, and Anthropology.* Baltimore: Johns Hopkins University Press.
Glueck, Grace. 1979. "Art People." *New York Times,* 16 February, C20.
Gómez-Peña, Guillermo. 1988. "Documented/Undocumented." In *Multi-Cultural Literacy,* ed. Rick Simonson and Scott Walker, 127–34. Saint Paul, Minn.: Greywolf Press.
Gordon, Ted, and Wahneema Lubiano. 1992. "The Statement of the Black Faculty Caucus." In *Debating P.C.: The Controversy over Political Correctness on College Campuses,* ed. Paul Berman, 249–57. New York: Laurel.
Gruen, John. 1979. "Jackie Winsor: Eloquence of a 'Yankee Pioneer.'" *Artnews,* March, 57–60.
Hamacher, Werner, Neil Hertz, and Thomas Keenan, eds. 1989. *Responses: On Paul de Man's Wartime Journalism.* Lincoln: University of Nebraska Press.

References

Haraway, Donna. 1992. "Ecce Homo, Ain't (Ar'n't) I a Woman, and Inappropriate/d Others: The Human in a Post-Humanist Landscape." *Feminists Theorize the Political*, ed. Judith Butler and Joan W. Scott, 86–100. New York: Routledge.
Harpham, Geoffrey Galt. 1992. *Getting It Right: Language, Literature, and Ethics*. Chicago: University of Chicago Press.
Heidegger, Martin. 1961. *An Introduction to Metaphysics*. Trans. Ralph Manheim. New York: Anchor Books.
———. 1977. "Letter on Humanism." In *Basic Writings of Martin Heidegger*, ed. David Farrell Krell. New York: Harper and Row.
Hughes, Robert. 1980. *The Shock of the New*. New York: Knopf.
———. 1992. "The Fraying of America." *Time*, 3 February, 44–49.
Huyssen, Andreas. 1986. *After the Great Divide: Modernism, Mass Culture, Postmodernism*. Bloomington: Indiana University Press.
Jameson, Fredric. 1992. *Signatures of the Visible*. New York: Routledge.
Jeffreys, Sheila. 1992. "Pornography and Creating the Sexual Future." *Ethics: A Feminist Reader*, ed. Elizabeth Frazer, Jennifer Hornsby, and Sabina Lovibond, 459–88. Oxford: Blackwell.
Kant, Immanuel. 1952. *The Critique of Judgement*. Trans. James Creed Meredith. Oxford: Oxford University Press.
———. 1969. *Foundations of the Metaphysics of Morals*. Trans. Lewis White Beck. Indianapolis: Bobbs-Merrill.
———. 1971. *The Doctrine of Virtue*. Trans. Mary J. Gregor. 1964. Reprint, Philadelphia: University of Pennsylvania Press.
———. 1983. *Perpetual Peace and Other Essays*. Trans. Ted Humphrey. Indianapolis: Hackett.
Kasper, M. 1992. *All Cotton Briefs*. 1985. Reprint, Brooklyn, N.Y.: Benzene.
Kimball, Roger. 1992. "The Periphery v. the Center: The MLA in Chicago." In *Debating P.C.: The Controversy over Political Correctness on College Campuses*, ed. Paul Berman, 61–84. New York: Laurel.
Kroeber, Karl. 1992. *Retelling/Rereading: The Fate of Storytelling in Modern Times*. New Brunswick, N.J.: Rutgers University Press.
Kurtz, Irma. 1993. "Agony Column." *Cosmopolitan*, August, 40–42.
Lacan, Jacques. 1977. *Écrits: A Selection*. Trans. Alan Sheridan. New York: Norton.
———. 1991. *Book 1: Freud's Papers on Technique, 1953–1954. The Seminar*. Trans. John Forrester. 1988. Reprint, New York: Norton.
———. 1992. *Book 7: The Ethics of Psychoanalysis. The Seminar*. Trans. Dennis Porter. New York: Norton.
Lévi-Strauss, Claude. 1961. *Race et histoire*. Paris: Éditions Gonthier.
———. 1977. *Tristes Tropiques*. Trans. John and Doreen Weightman. New York: Simon and Schuster.
———. 1983. *Le Regard éloigné*. Paris: Plon.
Lyotard, Jean-François. 1984. *The Postmodern Condition: A Report on Knowledge*. Trans. Geoff Bennington and Brian Massumi. Minneapolis: University of Minnesota Press.

References

———. 1988. *The Differend: Phrases in Dispute.* Trans. Georges Van Den Abbeele. Minneapolis: University of Minnesota Press.

———. 1989a. "Acinema." In *The Lyotard Reader,* ed. Andrew Benjamin, 169–80. Oxford: Blackwell.

———. 1989b. "Discussions; or, Phrasing 'after Auschwitz.'" In *The Lyotard Reader,* ed. Andrew Benjamin, 360–92. Oxford: Blackwell.

———. 1991. *The Inhuman: Reflections on Time.* Trans. Geoffrey Bennington and Rachel Bowlby. Stanford, Calif.: Stanford University Press.

MacCannell, Juliet Flower. 1991. *The Regime of the Brother: After the Patriarchy.* New York: Routledge.

MacKinnon, Catherine. 1992. "Privacy v. Equality: Beyond Roe v. Wade." In *Ethics: A Feminist Reader,* ed. Elizabeth Frazer, Jennifer Hornsby, and Sabina Lovibond, 351–63. Oxford: Blackwell.

McGrane, Bernard. 1989. *Beyond Anthropology: Society and the Other.* New York: Columbia University Press.

Melville, Herman. 1984. "Bartleby the Scrivener." In *Pierre; Israel Potter; The Piazza Tales; The Confidence Man; Uncollected Prose; Billy Budd, the Sailor.* New York: Library of America.

Miami Theory Collective. 1991. *Community at Loose Ends.* Minneapolis: University of Minnesota Press.

Mifflin, Margot. 1989. "Silent Character," *Elle,* November, 90.

Miller, J. Hillis. 1977. "The Critic as Host." *Critical Inquiry* 3:439–47.

———. 1986. "How Deconstruction Works." *New York Times Magazine,* 9 February, 25.

———. 1987. *The Ethics of Reading: Kant, de Man, Eliot, Trollope, James, and Benjamin.* New York: Columbia University Press.

———. 1990. *Versions of Pygmalion.* Cambridge, Mass.: Harvard University Press.

Nagel, Thomas. 1986. *The View from Nowhere.* New York: Oxford University Press.

Nietzsche, Friedrich. 1968. *The Will to Power.* Trans. Walter Kaufmann and R. J. Hollingdale. New York: Vintage.

———. 1969. *On the Genealogy of Morals.* Ed. and trans. Walter Kaufmann. New York: Vintage.

Pollitt, Katha. 1992. "Why Do We Read?" In *Debating P.C.: The Controversy over Political Correctness on College Campuses,* ed. Paul Berman, 201–11. New York: Laurel.

Rajchman, John. 1991. *Truth and Eros: Foucault, Lacan, and the Question of Ethics.* New York: Routledge.

Reed, Ishmael. 1988. "America: The Multicultural Society." In *Multi-Cultural Literacy,* ed. Rick Simonson and Scott Walker, 155–60. Saint Paul, Minn.: Greywolf Press.

———. 1989. "Ishmael Reed Talks about Multiculturalism, the Media, and Fighting Back." Interview by Keith Antar Mason. *High Performance* 12 (fall): 34–35.

References

Ricoeur, Paul. 1976. *Interpretation Theory: Discourse and the Surplus of Meaning.* Fort Worth: Texas Christian University Press.
———. 1981. "Narrative Time." In *On Narrative,* ed. W. J. T. Mitchell. 165–86. Chicago: University of Chicago Press.
Rorty, Richard. 1986. "On Ethnocentrism: A Reply to Clifford Geertz." *Michigan Quarterly Review* 25:525–34.
———. 1989a. "Education without Dogma: Truth, Freedom, and Our Universities." *Dissent* 36 (spring): 198–204.
———. 1989b. "From Ironist Theory to Private Allusions: Derrida." In *Contingency, Irony, and Solidarity.* Cambridge: Cambridge University Press.
———. 1991. *Philosophical Papers.* Volume 1: *Objectivity, Relativism, and Truth.* Volume 2: *Essays on Heidegger and Others.* Cambridge: Cambridge University Press.
Said, Edward W. 1992. "The Politics of Knowledge." In *Debating P.C.: The Controversy over Political Correctness on College Campuses,* ed. Paul Berman, 172–89. New York: Laurel.
Sartre, Jean-Paul. 1966. *Being and Nothingness.* Trans. Hazel E. Barnes. New York: Washington Square Press.
Schank, Roger C. 1990. *Tell Me a Story: A New Look at Real and Artificial Memory.* New York: Charles Scribner's Sons.
Searle, John. 1992. "The Storm over the University." In *Debating P.C.: The Controversy over Political Correctness on College Campuses,* ed. Paul Berman, 85–123. New York: Laurel.
Seidman, Steven. 1992. *Embattled Eros: Sexual Politics and Ethics in Contemporary America.* New York: Routledge.
Seung, T. K. 1982. *Semiotics and Thematics in Hermeneutics.* New York: Columbia University Press.
Shklar, Judith. 1984. *Ordinary Vices.* Cambridge, Mass: Harvard University Press.
———. 1994. "What Is the Use of Utopia?" In *Heterotopia: Postmodern Utopia and the Body Politic,* ed. Tobin Siebers, 40–57. Ann Arbor: University of Michigan Press.
Siebers, Tobin. 1983. *The Mirror of Medusa.* Berkeley and Los Angeles: University of California Press.
———. 1984. *The Romantic Fantastic.* Ithaca, N.Y.: Cornell University Press.
———. 1988. *The Ethics of Criticism.* Ithaca, N.Y.: Cornell University Press.
———. 1992. *Morals and Stories.* New York: Columbia University Press.
———. 1993. *Cold War Criticism and the Politics of Skepticism.* New York: Oxford University Press.
Smith, Barbara Herrnstein. 1981. "Narrative Versions, Narrative Theories." In *On Narrative,* ed. W. J. T. Mitchell, 209–32. Chicago: University of Chicago Press.

References

Smith, William Robertson. 1894. *Lectures on the Religion of the Semites*. London: A & C Black.
Sobel, Dean, ed. 1991. *Jackie Winsor*. Milwaukee: Milwaukee Art Museum.
Stimpson, Catharine R. 1992. "On Differences: Modern Language Association Presidential Address 1990." In *Debating P.C.: The Controversy Over Political Correctness on College Campuses*, ed. Paul Berman, 40–60. New York: Laurel.
Tallmer, Jerry. 1982. "The Sculpture That Went Boom." *New York Post*, 20 March.
Tomashevsky, Boris. 1965. "Thematics." In *Russian Formalist Criticism: Four Essays*, trans. Lee T. Lemon and Marion J. Reis, 61–95. Lincoln: University of Nebraska Press.
Wallace, Michele. 1991. "Multiculturalism and Oppositionality." *Afterimage* 19 (October): 6–9.
Weiskel, Portia Williams. 1976. "A Personal Introduction." In Thomas Weiskel. *The Romantic Sublime: Studies in the Structure and Psychology of Transcendence*. Baltimore: Johns Hopkins University Press.
Williams, Bernard. 1985. *Ethics and the Limits of Philosophy*. Cambridge, Mass.: Harvard University Press.
Winsor, Jackie. 1972. "An Interview with Jackie Winsor." Interview by Liza Bear. *Avalanche*, spring, 10–17.
———. 1986. "Interview with Jackie Winsor." Interview by Craig Gholson. *Bomb*, winter, 32–36.
Žižek, Slavoj. 1991. *Looking Awry: An Introduction to Jacques Lacan through Popular Culture*. Cambridge: MIT Press.

Index

Abortion, 22–24, 36
Aestheticism, 7, 51, 70
Aesthetic pleasure, 9–10
Aesthetics, 15, 21, 78, 107, 120, 131; defined, v, viii, 15, 116; and narrative, 26
Aesthetic taste, viii, 9, 46, 100
Affirmative action, 66
Afrocentrism, 66–67
Anthropology, vii, 47, 49, 52–53, 55–56, 58, 63, 71; moral status of, 47, 71; and Western tradition, 47, 49, 56–57, 67
Anti-ethnocentrism, 48–51, 67, 71, 75
Anuak, 52–53
Anzaldúa, Gloria, 73–74
Arendt, Hannah, 17–18, 25, 28, 119; on public sphere, 17–18
Aristotle, 2–3, 16, 19
Artifactual, 16–20
Art objects, viii, xi, 9, 11, 13–14, 17–18, 31, 38, 51, 69, 121
Artworld, 101–2
Auschwitz, viii, 72
Autonomy, x, 7–11, 16, 18, 81, 118, 129

Bad faith, 85, 95, 109
Barthes, Roland, ix, 77
Beauty, viii–ix, xi, 9, 10–12, 14–16, 18, 99, 107, 108, 113–14, 116–17, 120–21, 129; distrust of, viii; feminist critique of, 108; moral symbolism of, 8–9; and objectification, 9; and politics, xi, 113; smallness of, 114
Blanchot, Maurice, 85, 88
Bloom, Allan, 67–68, 70
Booth, Wayne, vi, 80
Butler, Judith, 6–7

Capitalism, 33–34
Castoriadis, Cornelius, 8, 20, 27, 46, 119, 130
Categorical imperative, 127–29
Cavell, Stanley, 100–101, 119
Character, xi, 66, 87, 92–94, 105, 106, 116, 120–21, 131; defined, 120
Civil rights, 65–66, 70, 73
Civil rights movement, 65, 73
Cold war, xi, 31, 33
Comedy, 1, 28
Communism, 33–34
Community, 17, 20–21, 26, 28, 35, 38, 46, 55–59, 61, 63, 65, 80, 116, 129; as artifactual, viii, 21, 31, 38, 46; and ethic of the victim, 64, 69; in ethics, 48, 55, 80, 116; and free speech, 21; and individual responsibility, 20–21, 118, 129; and interpretation, 27; as morally unsatisfying, xi; narrative dimension of, 26, 46; and objectivity,

Index

Community (*continued*)
60; in politics, viii, 48, 58, 75, 132; and romantic couple, 36–37, 108; and women, 22, 24
Consensus, vi, viii, 13, 17–20, 60–61, 113, 120, 129
Cosmopolitanism, 47, 54, 57, 59, 72, 75–76; and colonialism, 54; defined, 47
Cosmopolitan morality, 51–52, 69, 71–72
Culler, Jonathan, 55

D'Souza, Dinesh, 65–67
Danto, Arthur, 15
De Man, Paul, 12–13, 79, 93–94, 119; and ethicity, 12
Death, 118, 123, 130
Deconstruction, 12–13, 27, 78–79, 82–83, 85, 89, 94, 119; and self-refutation, 27
Definition, vi–vii, xii, 37, 58, 117
Democracy, v, 8, 19, 24–25, 33–34, 51, 71–72, 124–25
Derrida, Jacques, vii, 11–12, 14, 77, 119
Desire, ix, 5, 29–31, 94–98, 101, 103, 111
Diary disease, 70, 74
Disagreement, 13, 135
Diversity, 49–52, 54, 69, 80; as an aesthetic object, 51
Durkheim, Émile, 58, 122

Enlightenment, v, x, xi, 30, 35, 60, 70, 81
Equality, viii, 17–18, 34–36, 62, 110
Erotics, 15, 106
Ethical conflict, viii, 4, 12, 16
Ethic of the victim, 63–65
Ethics, vi, viii, 1, 8, 12, 116, 120, 122, 133; defined, vii, 2, 48, 116; dominance of, 28, 132; and law, 64; vs. morality, 1; and narrative, 26; nausea of, viii, xii, 2, 4, 7–9, 14–15; vs. politics, 48, 116, 126–29; and repetition, 2; and sexuality, 104, 106; and solidarity, 55; and subjectivity, 132; and textuality, 12
Ethics of reading, 13–14, 79–80, 85, 87–89, 92–93
Ethnocentrism, 47, 49, 51, 56–57, 59–60, 63, 75; and objectivity, 58
Evans-Pritchard, E. E., 52–53, 74
Existentialism, 74, 95, 118
Experience, vii, 28; repeatability of, vii, 1

Family, 22, 36–37, 108
Feminism, 6, 16, 21–24, 35, 77, 108–9. *See also* Women's movement
Foucault, Michel, 3, 19, 95, 106
Frederick William II, 124–25
Freedom, x, xi, 8–9, 27, 76, 81, 109, 114, 118, 125, 127, 130–32, 135; defined, 118; in Kant, 118, 128; and objectification, 9
Freedom of expression, 20; defined, 20
Freedom of speech, 18–20, 65, 124; and community, 20; defined, 18
Freud, Sigmund, xi, 1, 2, 30, 35, 94–98, 100, 103, 110, 133
Friendship, 16, 122; sexualization of, 16

Gans, Eric, vii, 130
Gay and lesbian rights, 24, 37
Gaze, 110–11
Geertz, Clifford, 49, 50–58, 60, 74; on anthropological ethics, 49
Gender, vi, xi, 6, 21–22, 35, 62, 73, 80
Girard, René, vii, 130
Grand narratives, 3, 13, 30, 32, 35, 60–61

Haraway, Donna, 6–7, 31
Harpham, Geoffrey Galt, 3–4, 7, 14

Index

Harris v. McRae, 23–24. *See also* Abortion
Hegel, G. W. F., x, 1
Heidegger, Martin, xi, 2–4, 93, 95–98, 100, 105, 110, 114
History, 1–3, 7, 15, 28, 106, 108; and repetition, 1–2; and sexuality, 15; and subjectivity, x
Holocaust, viii
Hughes, Robert, 32, 64
Human conflict, vii, 4–5, 10, 12–14, 34, 46, 123–24, 134; and ethics, viii, xi, 2–3; and repetition, 2, 5, 10, 12
Husserl, Edmund, v, 132
Huyssen, Andreas, 29, 34

Identification, xi, 87–88, 93–94, 116, 134
Identity, v, vii, 6, 103, 131–33; defined, 134
Instinct, 96, 103–4, 108, 111
Intercultural distinctions, 48, 57, 72, 74
Interpretation, 27
Intracultural distinctions, 48, 72

James, Henry, 78, 84, 92–93
Jameson, Fredric, 31, 96

Kant, Immanuel, x, xii, 8–10, 13, 75, 79, 81, 97, 111, 115, 117, 119–20, 123–25, 127–30, 132; on autonomy, 8–9, 11, 16, 81, 118; on the sublime, 107
Kroeber, Karl, 25–26, 46

Lacan, Jacques, 2, 5, 10–11, 88, 95, 97, 103, 110–12
Lévi-Strauss, Claude, 49, 53–54, 56, 103
Liberal individualism, 16, 22
Literary characters, 78, 88, 94; relation to their authors, 86, 88, 92
Lyotard, Jean-François, viii, 3, 13, 32, 60–61, 72, 98, 99, 100, 102, 105

MacKinnon, Catharine, 22–23
Marx, Karl, 1–2, 59
Masochism, 16, 99
McGrane, Bernard, 52, 137
Melville, Herman, 84, 88, 92; "Bartleby the Scrivener," 13, 84–85, 89, 91–92
Miller, J. Hillis, vi, xi, 13, 78–94
Modernism, 30, 32–33, 36, 38, 46
Modernity, 31–34, 102
Moral description, 4–5
Moral disgust, viii, 4, 7, 9–10, 26, 75, 84
Moral dissatisfaction, viii, 9, 11, 14, 17, 30
Moral experience, 1, 5–6; and time, 5
Multiculturalism, xi, 34, 47–48, 57, 62–70, 74; and aesthetics, 69–70; and anthropological tradition, 63; defined, 47; and racism, 63, 66–67

Nachträglichkeit, 5
Nagel, Thomas, 8
Narrative, ix, 12–13, 25–26, 32, 38, 46, 60–61, 79, 85–86, 88–89, 93–94; and conflict, 4, 12, 14; defined, 25–26; and personification, 78–79, 83, 84–88, 90–91, 94; and repetition, vii, ix, 14, 26–28
National Socialism, 4, 61, 114
Nausea, viii, xi, 1–10, 12, 14–15, 17, 28, 34, 84, 136
Newman, Barnett, 99–100, 105, 107
Nietzsche, Friedrich, 1, 11, 86, 92
Nonviolence, 58, 72
Nostalgia, 2–3

Objectification, ix, xi–xii, 9–11, 110, 118, 132–34; and aesthetics, 9, 132; and conflict, 10; and repetition, 10; and subjectivity, xi, 78, 133, 134

Index

Objectivity, x, 52, 54–55, 57–61, 65–66, 75–76, 117
Objet petit a, 110
Obscenity, 95–96, 98–100, 103, 108, 111; defined, 96; and denaturing of sexual act, 96; and the gaze, 110; and meaning, 96; and modern thought, 95, 111; and representation, 96; and sadomasochism, 99
Otherness, 30, 34, 50, 53, 56, 61, 69, 94, 115; as alternative to us, 49, 53, 55

Peace, 116–17, 121–22
Personhood, ix, 84, 91–92, 105, 132
Personification, ix, 78, 83, 84–85, 93–94. *See also* Prosopopoeia
Politics, vi, viii, 7, 15, 25, 31, 55, 64, 75, 119, 122, 132; and aesthetics, 8, 17, 21, 35, 129; and the artificial, 17; defined, viii, 16, 22, 48, 116, 121; and narrative, 26, 38, 46; and symbolism, 121; as tragic space, 20, 124, 126, 130, 135
Pollock, Jackson, 107
Pornography, 20–21, 23, 100–103
Posering, 99, 100, 102, 105
Postmodernism, xi, 3, 5–8, 10, 15–17, 29–38, 41, 46, 49–50, 53, 60–61, 95, 116; defined, 32; and feminism, 35; and the political, 33; and the postwar, 31
Privacy, 22–24
Private sphere, 17–19, 23–24
Prosopopoeia, xi, 77–79, 83–87, 90, 92, 94. *See also* Personification
Psychoanalysis, 5, 11, 94–95, 103, 111
Public sphere, 17–25, 135; feminist critique of, 22; vs. private sphere, 17–18, 20–21, 23; and symbolism, 18, 35
Publicity, 20, 128–29

Race, vi, 26, 63, 66, 73, 80
Rajchman, John, 5, 11–12, 19, 106
Rawls, John, 3, 75
Reading for character, xi, 87–88, 92–93
Religion, 116, 120, 122
Repetition, vii, viii, ix, 1–12, 14–15, 24–26, 28–29, 38, 83, 84–85; and experience, vii, 2, 14, 26, 28; and nausea, xi, 1–2, 4, 7, 9–11, 28; and style, 11; and time, 5
Rereading, 14, 25
Ricoeur, Paul, 25
Roe v. Wade, 23–24. *See also* Abortion
Romantic couple, 16, 36–37
Romanticism, 30, 35–36
Rorty, Richard, 11, 49, 50–55, 58–62, 65, 71–72, 75
Rothko, Mark, 107
Rousseau, Jean-Jacques, 36, 56, 77, 135

Sadomasochism, 100, 106, 112
Said, Edward, 63, 73
Sartre, Jean-Paul, x, 74, 82, 109–10
Schank, Roger, 27–28
Self, x, 3, 7, 16, 32, 69, 77–78, 86–87, 98, 108, 117, 134; and aesthetics, 68, 77–78; and anthropology, 56; and autonomy, x, 118, 131; in Kant, 8; multicultural, 69; and objectification, 78, 133–34; and objects of consciousness, v, vii, 132; and personification, 83, 86. *See also* Subject
Self and other, 16, 55–56, 74–75, 115–17, 127, 129
Self-reflection, 7–10, 16, 129
Sexual couple. *See* Romantic couple
Sexual desire, 98, 102, 110
Sexual difference, 35, 36, 107–8
Sexual politics, 16, 25, 36–37
Sexuality, xi, 15, 25, 35–36, 95, 97–98, 104, 106, 108, 110
Shklar, Judith, 36–37

Solidarity, 2, 26, 52–55, 59–61, 65, 69, 75–76; and the aesthetic, 69; vs. objectivity, 52

Style, 11–13, 15; and moral conflict, 12–13; and sex, 15

Subject, v, vii, viii, ix–xii, 6, 8, 16, 56, 75, 78, 83–84, 87–88, 95–96, 99, 102–3, 106, 108, 116–17, 131–35; and aesthetics, v; and autonomy, x, 8–9; beautiful, 108; and becoming, ix; bourgeois, v; defined, v, 132, 134–35; democratic, v; and emancipation, x; and ethics, 116, 132–33; and experience, 81; instability of, ix; and nothingness, x; and objectification, 132–33; and objects of consciousness, 83, 132; and reason, 81; skepticism about, x; split, 8, 98; sublime, 99, 102–3, 116. *See also* Self

Subjectivization, v, x, 78

Sublime, xi, 9, 11, 95, 97–99, 101–3, 106–8, 113–14; vs. beauty, xi, 103, 107, 113–14; classical, 102, 106, 107, 108; defined, 9, 10, 97–98, 120; and ethics, 9; and instinct, 103; and loss, 100; mathematical, 10, 126; modern, 102, 108, 113; and power, 103; and religion, 116, 120, 129; and romantic couple, 107; and sadomasochism, 112; and sexuality, 97, 103, 106, 108; and subjectivity, 99; and virility, 107

Supercommunity, 57, 59–60, 72

Symbolic violence, 74–75

Totalitarianism, 33–34, 134

Transference, 10–11

Utopia, x, 9, 12, 30–32, 36, 46, 60, 72–73, 116; and aesthetics, 12, 38; classical, 36; vs. dystopia, 31; and ethics, 116; and ethnocentrism, 60; and exclusion, 116; in modern theory, 31; narrative, 4; as political good, 116; and postmodernism, xi, 30, 31, 35, 38, 46; and sexuality, 15, 36, 107; and time, 31

Victim's rights, 64, 65

Violence, vii–viii, x, 19, 57, 61, 75, 83, 89, 113, 124, 128, 130, 132; and beauty, viii; and community, 55, 126; and democracy, 125; and ethics, 64; fear of, xi, 37, 124, 135; in Foucault, 106; and history, 1; and individuality, 129; intracultural, 74; in Kant, 129; male, 108; and narrative, 89; and symbolic violence, 74–75; and virility, 108

Virtue, 20, 82, 89, 107, 116, 120, 127, 130

West, 47, 49, 50, 52, 56, 68, 74

Williams, Bernard, vi, 3, 8

Winsor, Jackie, xi, 32, 38–39, 41, 43; *Exploded Piece*, 41, 43; *Green Piece*, 39, 43; *Painted Piece*, 39, 41, 43

Women's movement, 22–24. *See also* Feminism

Žižek, Slavoj, 110–12